# MEDIEVAL BI

## in the Sherborne Missa

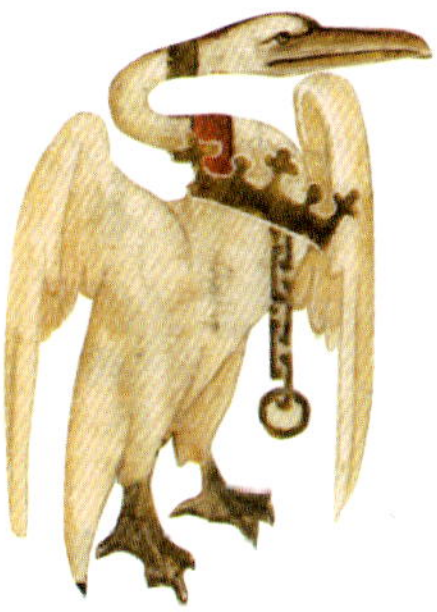

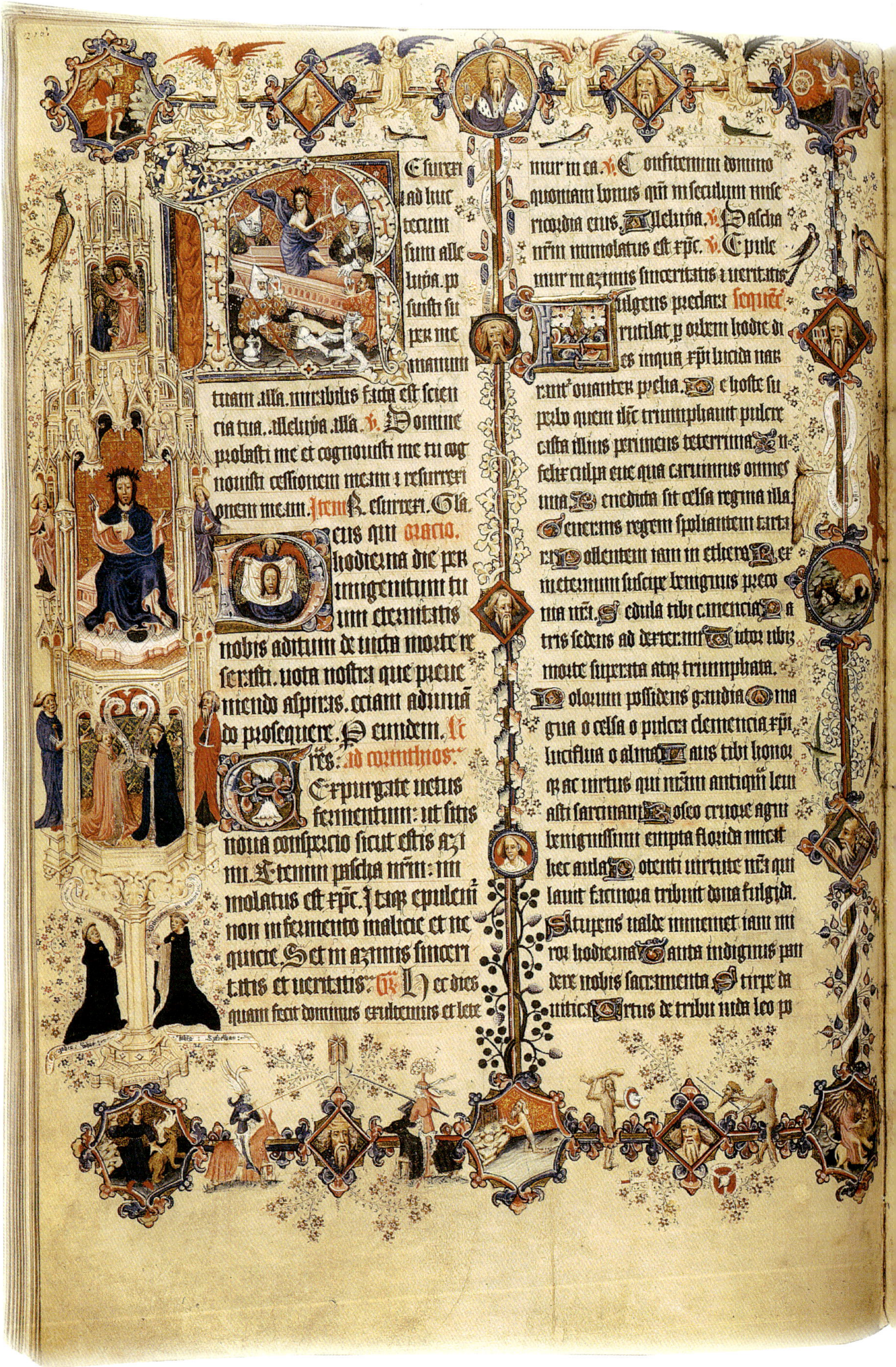

# MEDIEVAL BIRDS
## in the Sherborne Missal

JANET BACKHOUSE

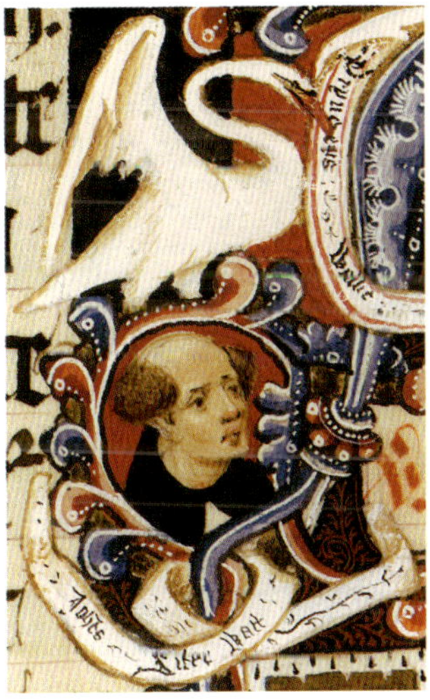

THE BRITISH LIBRARY

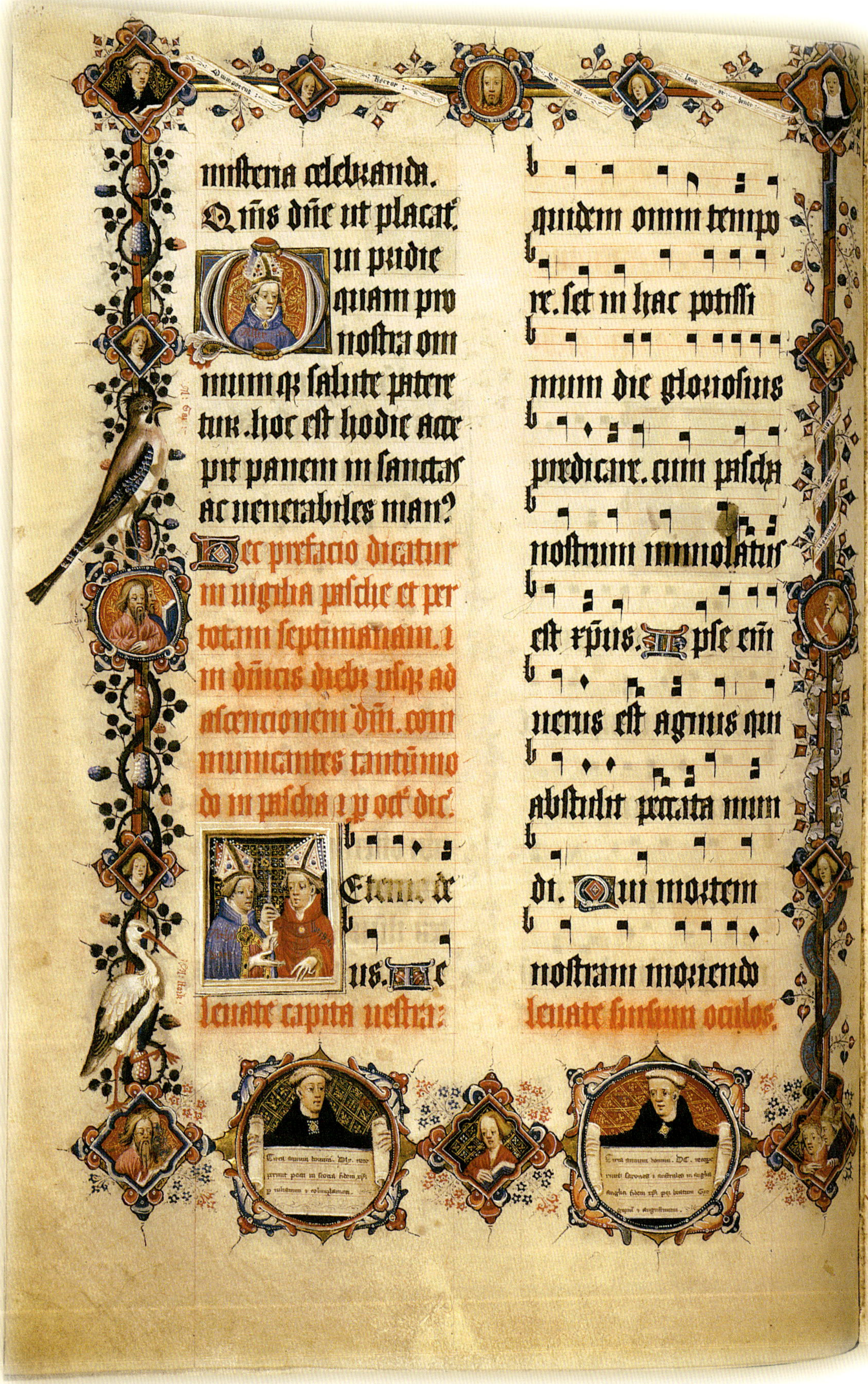
misteria celebranda.
Quis dñe ut placat
Qui pridie
quam pro
nostra om
nium q3 salute pater
tur. hoc est hodie acce
pit panem in sanctas
ac venerabiles man?
Hec prefacio dicitur
in vigilia pasche et per
totam septimanam. et
in dñicis diebus usqz ad
ascensionem dñi. com
municantes tantummo
do in pascha et per oct' dic.
Et enim d
us. Le
levate capita vestra:
quidem omni tempo
re. set in hac potissi
mum die gloriosius
predicare. cum pascha
nostrum immolatus
est xpus. Ipse enim
verus est agnus qui
abstulit peccata mun
di. Qui mortem
nostram moriendo
levate sursum oculos.

# INTRODUCTION

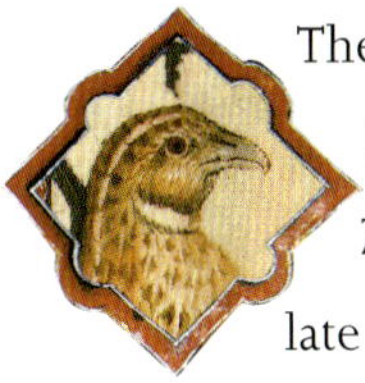

The Sherborne Missal, purchased for the nation in 1998 with the aid of the National Heritage Memorial Fund and now numbered Additional MS 74326 in the British Library, is one of the outstanding masterpieces of late medieval English book painting. Written and illuminated at the very beginning of the 15th century for the Benedictine abbey of Sherborne in Dorset, its pages are lavishly ornamented with an astonishing range of pictorial themes, some devotional, others historical, linked by motifs which are apparently purely decorative in intention. Among the latter is the already celebrated sequence of forty-eight naturalistic images of British birds, the majority of them identified by name in Middle English. No comparable series appears in any known European manuscript of the period. Individual examples of these birds have already been reproduced in contexts both scholarly and popular. One or two of them have been widely circulated on greetings cards. This is, however, the first time that they have been published as a complete series in full colour.

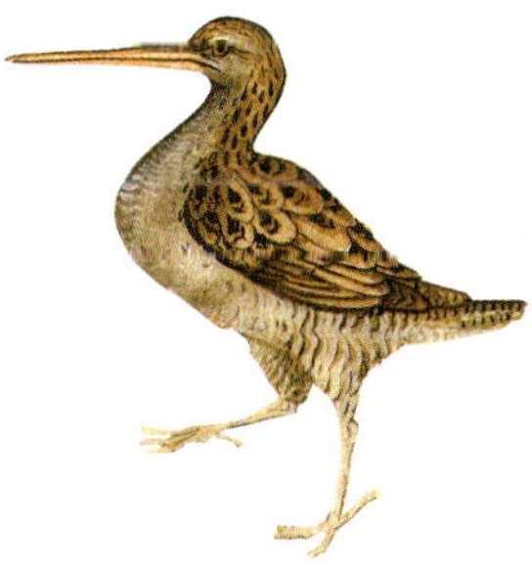

1 *A complete page from the manuscript, showing a range of decoration which includes bishops of Sherborne, episodes from church history and marginal figures of the jay and the stork, (p. 366).*

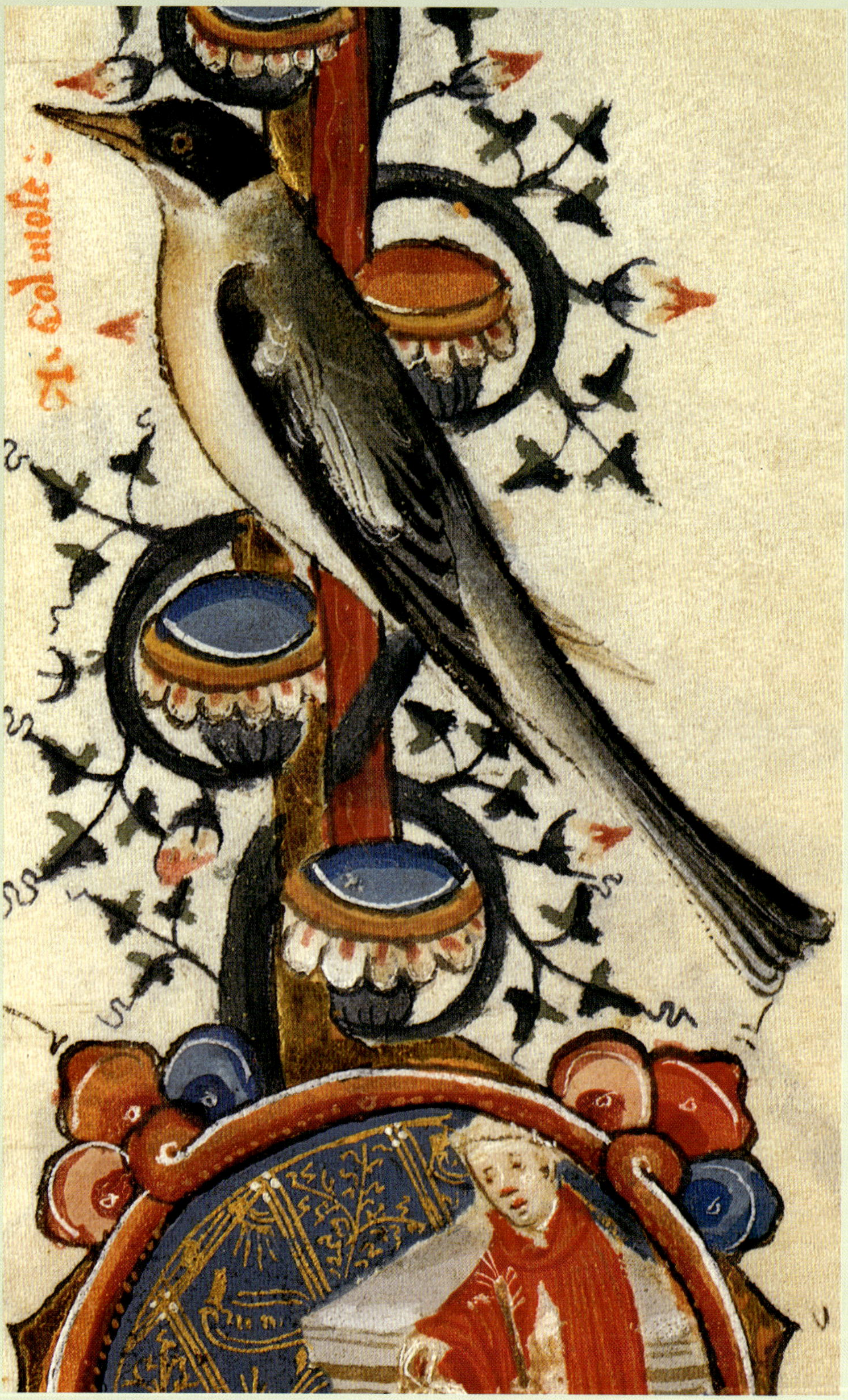

# BIRDS IN MANUSCRIPTS

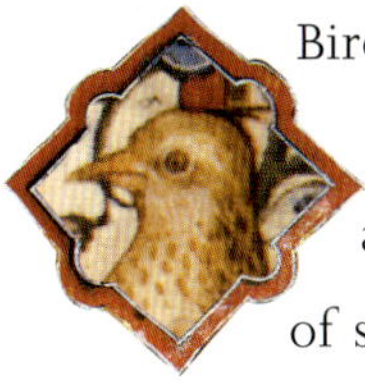

Birds appear in illuminated manuscripts in a wide variety of styles and contexts during the whole of the Middle Ages. They are to be found as illustrations to various books of the Bible, as accessories to the lives of saints, as characters in fables and story cycles, as subjects in scientific and practical works, as heraldic and otherwise symbolic devices, and simply as decorative motifs included to enliven the empty margins of the written page. In many instances no actual species is distinguishable. In others, though certain features

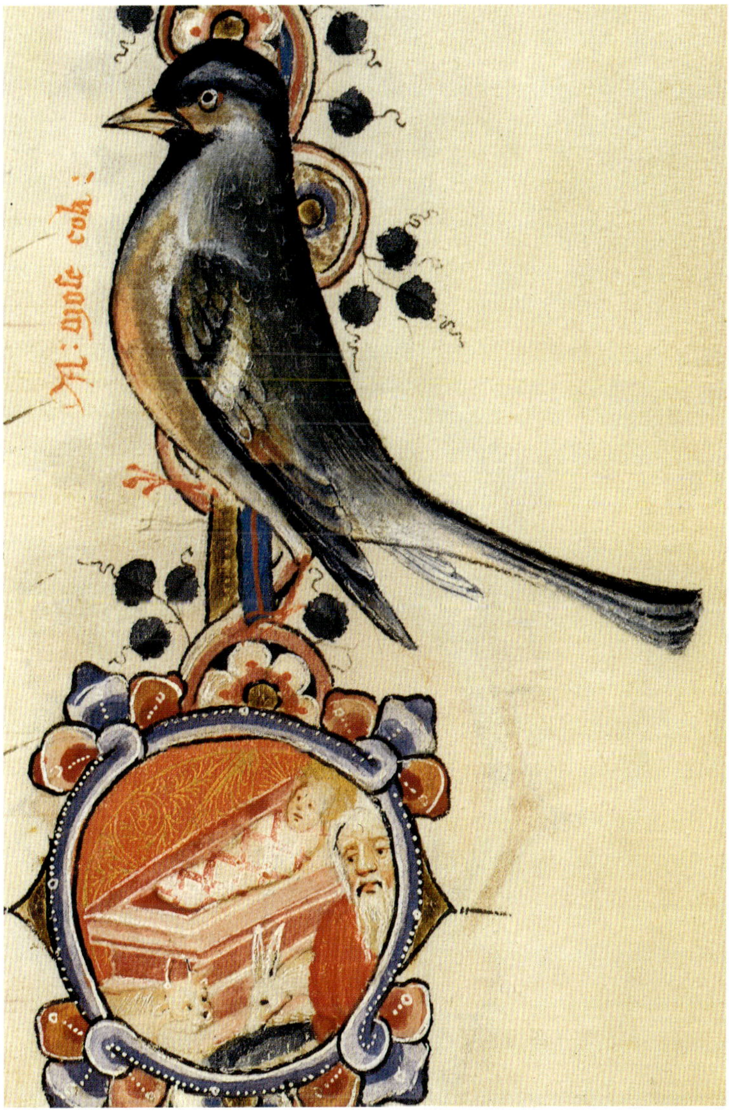


2 *A mose cok*: possibly intended to represent a great tit, (p.363, *above*).

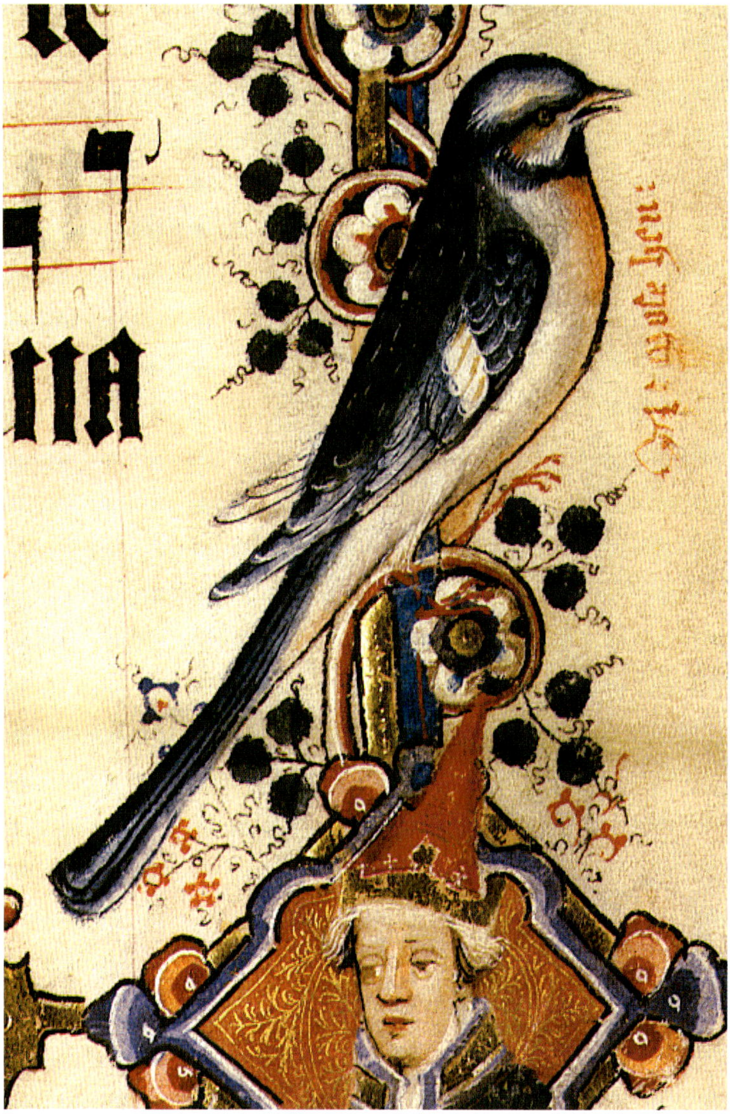

3 *A mose hen: probably a blue tit,* *(p. 363, below).*

of an identifiable bird may be faithfully and accurately rendered, the whole is too strongly coloured by the stylistic idiom of the period which produced it to be regarded as a true likeness of its subject.

During the early Middle Ages, the Latin Bestiary was the basic source of information about living creatures. The text, much of it fabulous and presented with a moralistic slant, was drawn largely from classical sources, its chief foundation being the Physiologus, which was in existence before the 5th century. In the 12th and 13th centuries, bestiaries were extremely popular and numerous copies were richly illustrated to order. Although they tend to be overshadowed by

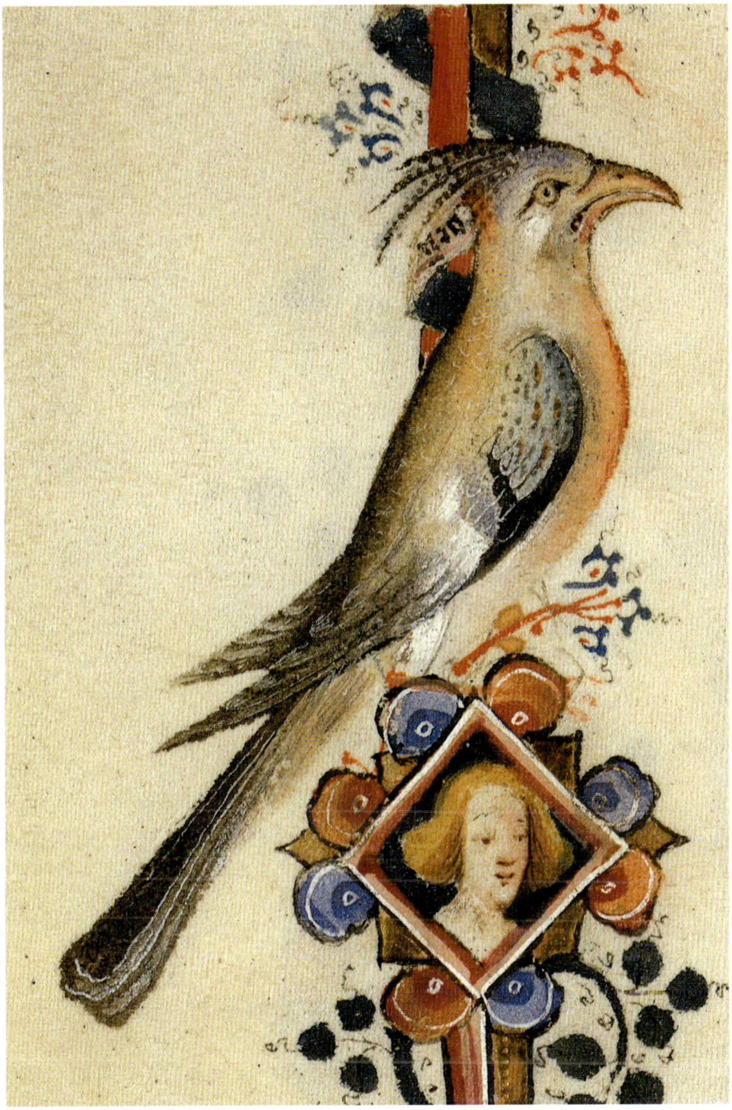

4 *Unidentified bird: probably imaginary,* (p. 364, *above*).

animal subjects, as many as twenty different birds may be included in these manuscripts, among them such familiar species as the heron, the swan, the owl and the swallow, often inspiring remarkably accurate images. Various collections of animal and bird fables, notably those of Aesop, were also circulated and, at least in the later Middle Ages, attracted illustration in copies intended for the libraries of the well-to-do.

Birds are familiar in many devotional contexts. The Third Person of the Holy Trinity is traditionally portrayed in the guise of a bird, though not always instantly recognisable as the dove which it is intended to be. The fourth evangelist, St John, is symbolised from earliest times by an eagle. Illustrations to well-known biblical episodes, including the Creation, the story of Noah, and the apocalyptic calling of the birds, are rich sources of bird iconography. Bird stories frequently feature in the lives of saints. The best known is probably that of St Francis of Assissi preaching to the birds, but other holy men, including the English St Cuthbert of Lindisfarne, are associated with bird miracles which inspire illustrations in copies of their lives.

On a more purely practical level, treatises on hunting would be incomplete without material on hawking, which was a widespread activity. This was also a frequent subject among the miniatures of the occupations of the months, with which the calendars of psalters and book of hours were habitually decorated.

The higher classes of society who most frequently enjoyed this sport would also have been routinely familiar with bird imagery in the context of heraldry and livery badges, such as the famous swan device used by the Bohun earls of Hereford, maternal ancestors of King Henry V (see half-title page).

The purely decorative use of birds in English illuminated manuscripts has a very long history. The earliest known example is the Lindisfarne Gospels, produced in Northumbria at the very end of the 7th century and associated with the shrine of St Cuthbert. Many of its pages feature elaborate and sinuous bird forms, entwined into complicated patterns. Their curved beaks, exaggerated talons and stylised plumage place them firmly in the realms of fantasy, but their forms and attitudes suggest that their creator had absorbed his raw material through daily familiarity with the rich and varied bird life still to be enjoyed on and around the coast of north-east England. Later artists were to feature individual bird images in their marginal schemes. They are particularly characteristic of 13th and 14th century work on either side of the English Channel, in both devotional and secular books, and specific types of bird are frequently recognisable. However, although other manuscripts may offer a wide variety of bird imagery, nowhere else do we find a programme as deliberate and sustained as that included in the illustration of the Sherborne Missal.

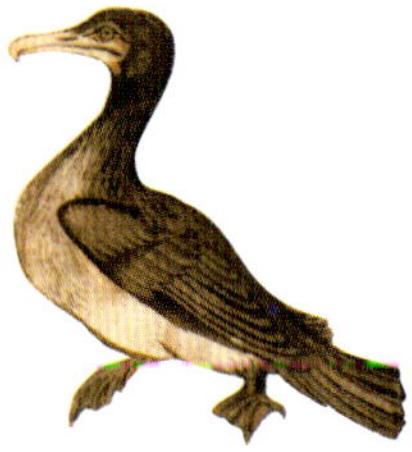

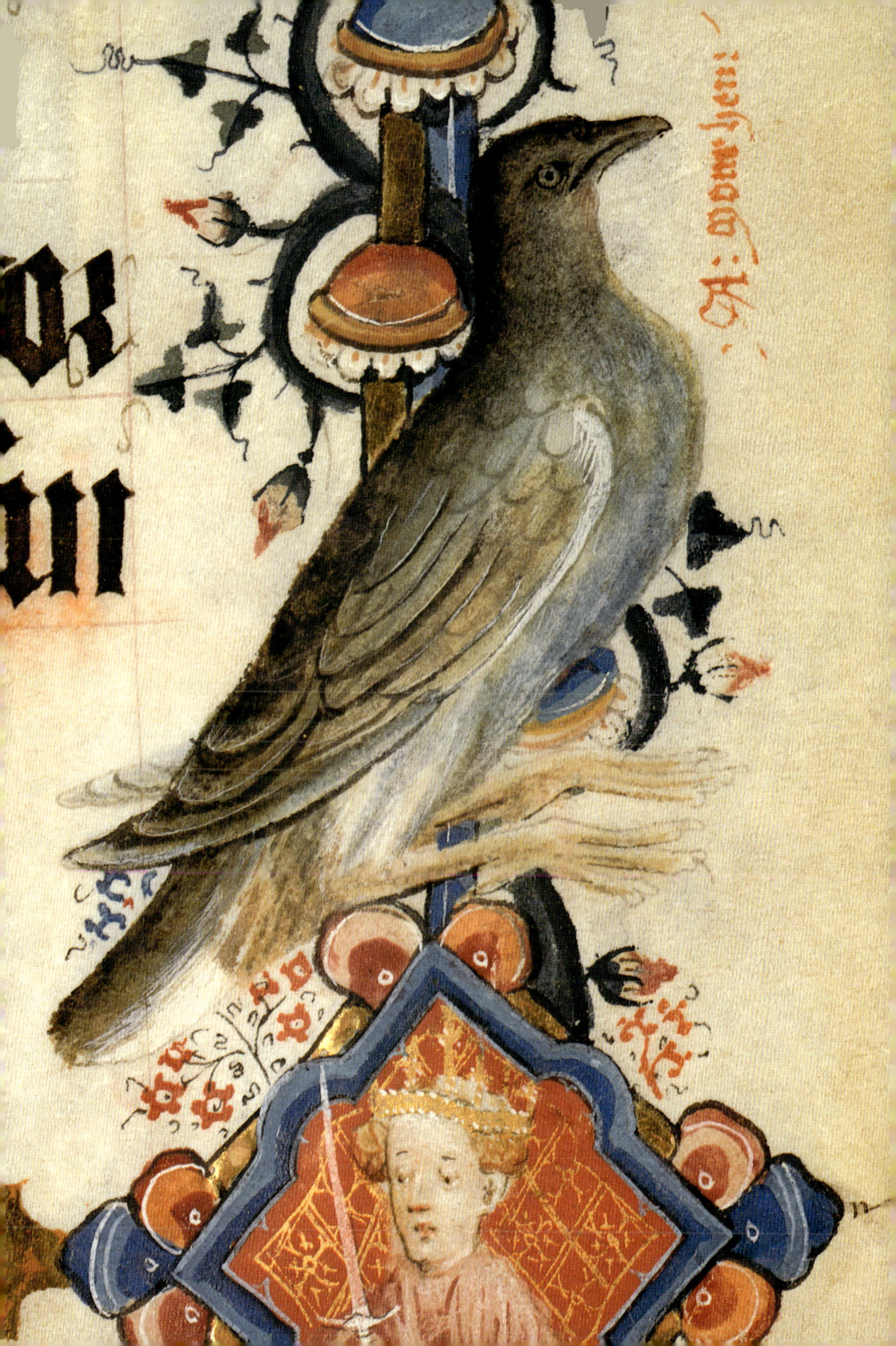

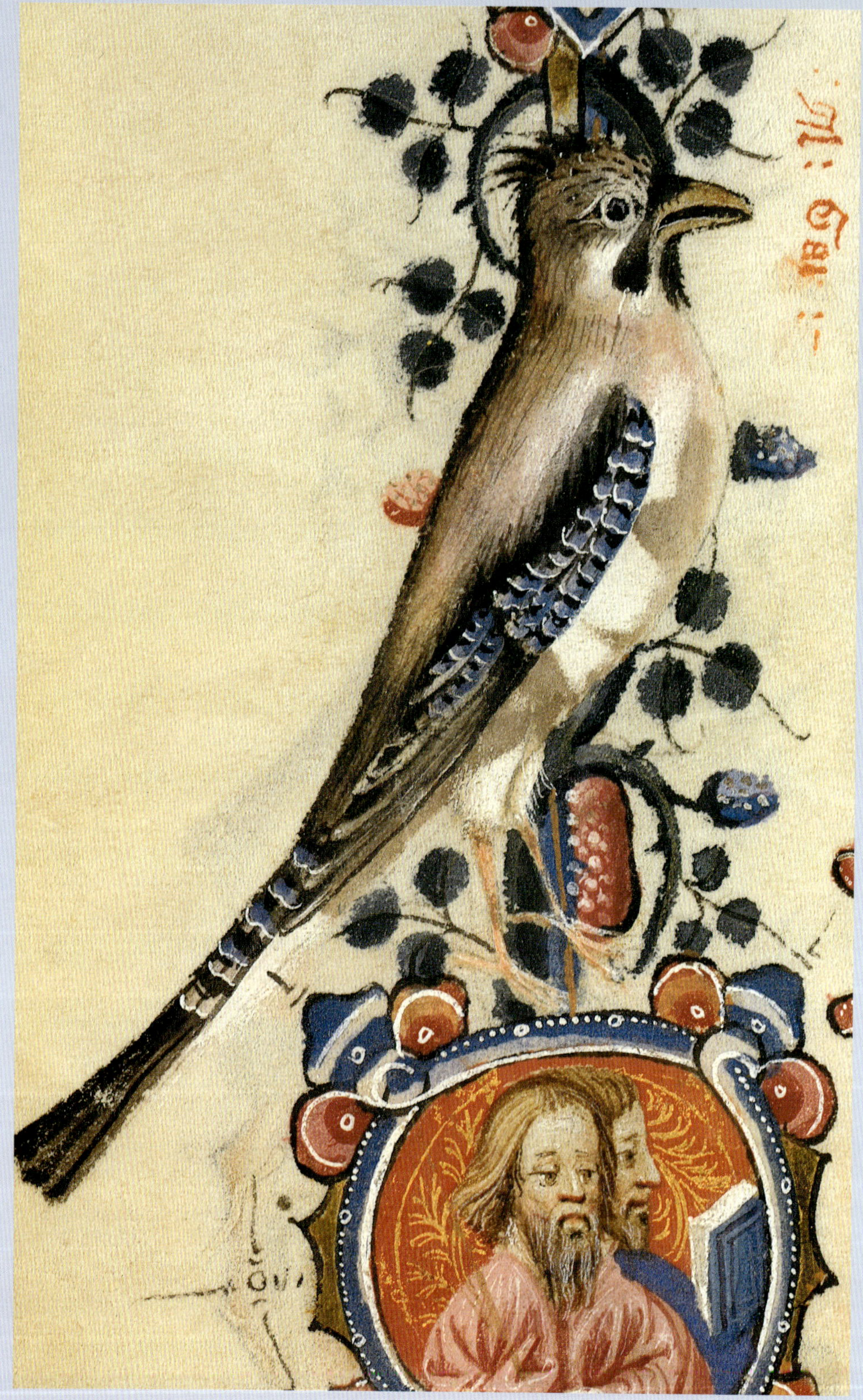

# THE MISSAL AND ITS MAKERS

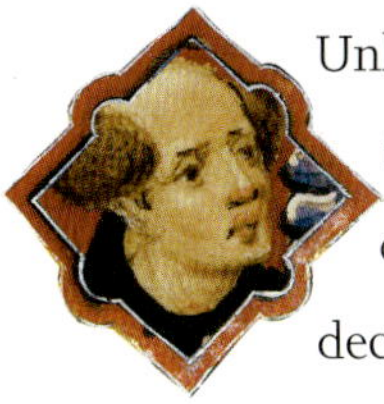

Unlike many of the major illuminated books which have come down to us from the Middle Ages, the Sherborne Missal can be both localised and dated with a remarkable degree of accuracy. Details of both text and decoration offer firm evidence of its association with the Benedictine abbey of Sherborne in Dorset. The abbot responsible for its creation is portrayed on many of its pages and can be identified as Robert Brunyng, elected to the position in 1385. He died in 1415, the year of the battle of Agincourt. In several places he is accompanied by the contemporary bishop of Salisbury, Richard Mitford (or Medford), who occupied the see from 1396 until 1407. The Missal must therefore have been made while Mitford was bishop. Both the scribe and the principal illuminator are also named and portrayed within the manuscript. The scribe was a Benedictine monk called John Whas of whom nothing, beyond his name, is certainly known. He must, however, have been a member of the Sherborne community because he would have needed access to textual models within the house as sources for his task. The illuminator was a Dominican friar, John Siferwas, who must have been called in from elsewhere for the sake of his artistic expertise. A few documentary references to him have been traced and his name appears in another manuscript of the period, a gospel lectionary (now Harley MS 7026 in the British Library) presented to the cathedral of Salisbury by John Lord Lovel, who died in 1408. Stylistic analysis of the Missal shows that several different artists worked on its decoration but Siferwas may be presumed to have been the guiding hand. Both Whas and Siferwas are portrayed several times in the manuscript, distinguishable by their monastic habits, the one in Benedictine black and the other in the black mantle and white habit of the Dominicans.

All four figures – bishop, abbot, scribe and illuminator – may be seen on the page introducing the mass for Easter Sunday (see frontispiece), in the left-hand margin below the figure of the Resurrected Christ. This is one of the places in which both Whas and Siferwas are named. In one of his other named appearances (see title page), Siferwas is placed alongside a shield of arms of the Prince of Wales, accompanied by the swan emblem of the Bohun family. This can only refer to the young Henry V during his father's reign. As Henry IV did not become king until the autumn of 1399, it offers further evidence of a very close dating for the manuscript as a whole.

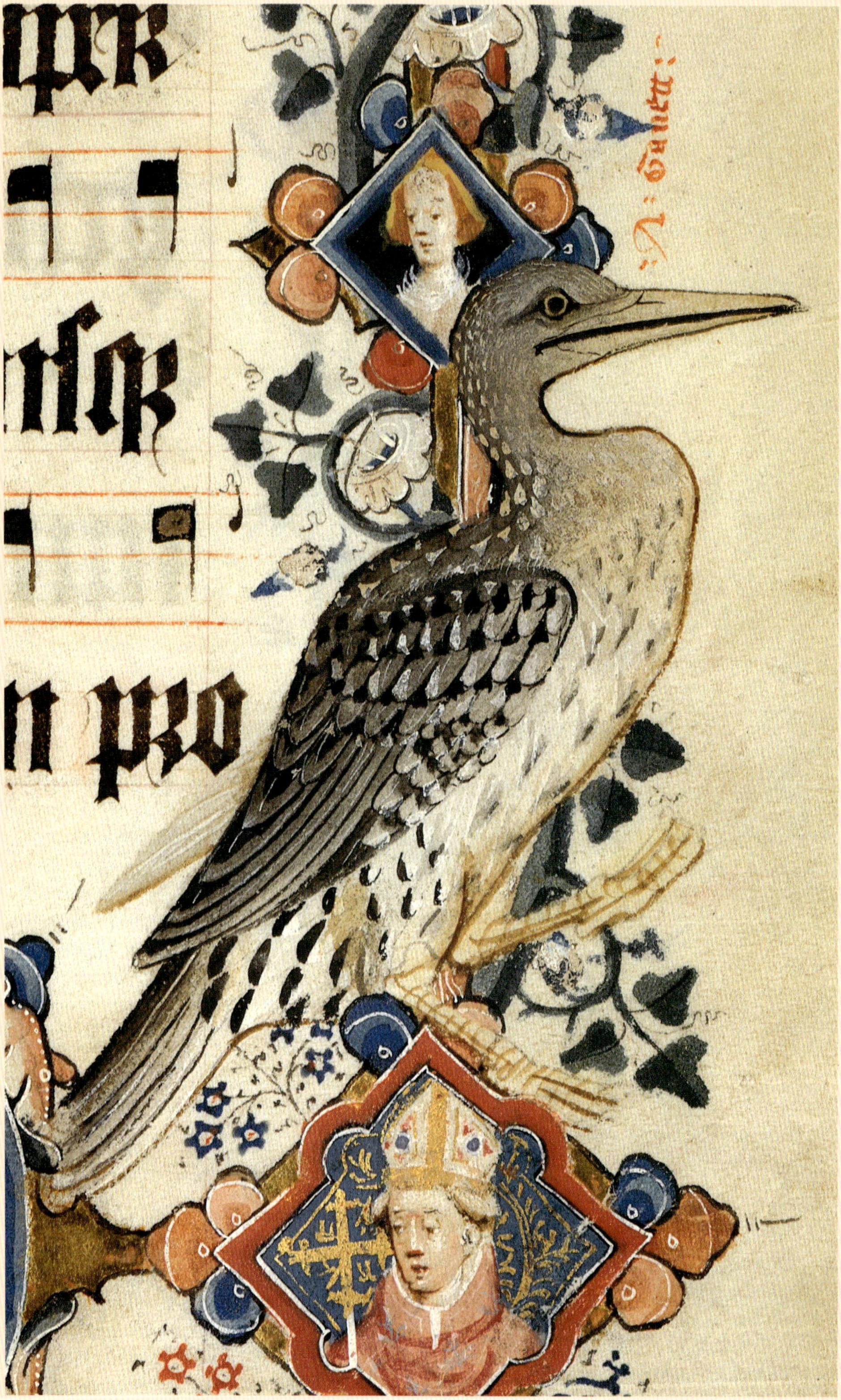

# THE CONTENT OF THE MISSAL AND THE PLACING OF THE BIRDS

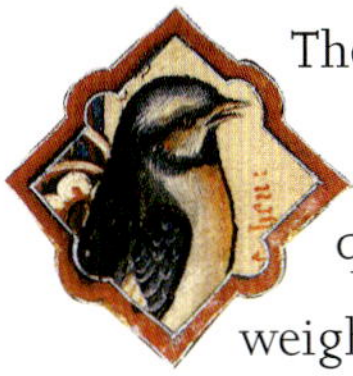

The Sherborne Missal is by any standards an extremely large and impressive book. Made up of 347 leaves (694 pages) of stout, good quality vellum, each measuring 21 x 15 inches (53.5 x 38 cm), and weighing well over 40 pounds, it contains all the texts necessary for the

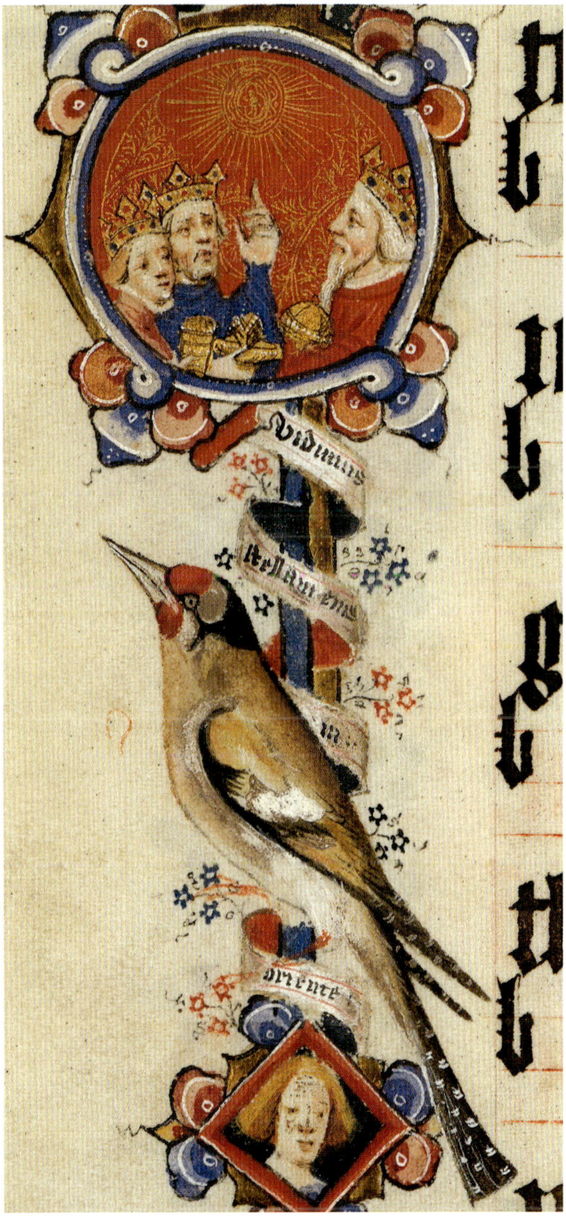

*5 Unidentified bird: a goldfinch, (p. 364, below).*

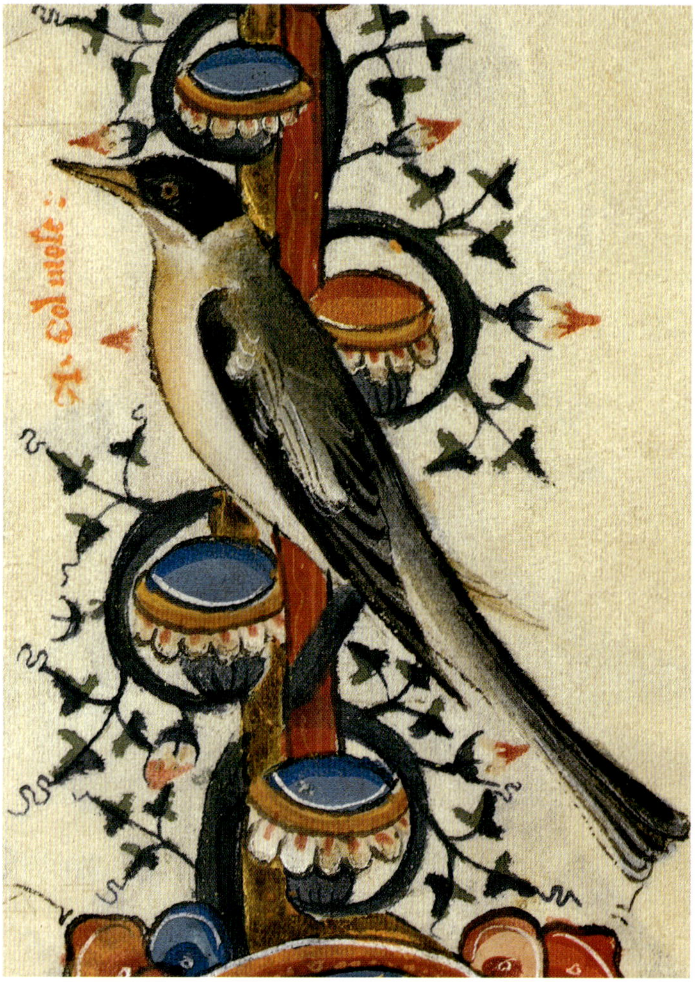

6 *A Col mose: a coal tit,* (p. 365, *above*). Enlargement on p. 6.

celebration of mass on every day of the liturgical year. Preceded by a calendar in which the annual sequence of saints' days is recorded, the content of the book is arranged in three sections. First comes the *Temporale*, composed of material for the yearly cycle based on the principal events in the life of Christ, beginning with the season of Advent, which leads into the major festival of Christmas. The *Sanctorale*, comprising material for the feasts of individual saints, is in third position, ending with a series of votive masses for such special intentions as the welfare of the sick. Between *Temporale* and *Sanctorale* is the text not subject to seasonal or daily change, centred on the prayers recited at the consecration of the bread and the wine at the heart of the mass.

The team responsible for the production of the Missal intended from the first that it should be a manuscript of exceptional grandeur, in which the maximum

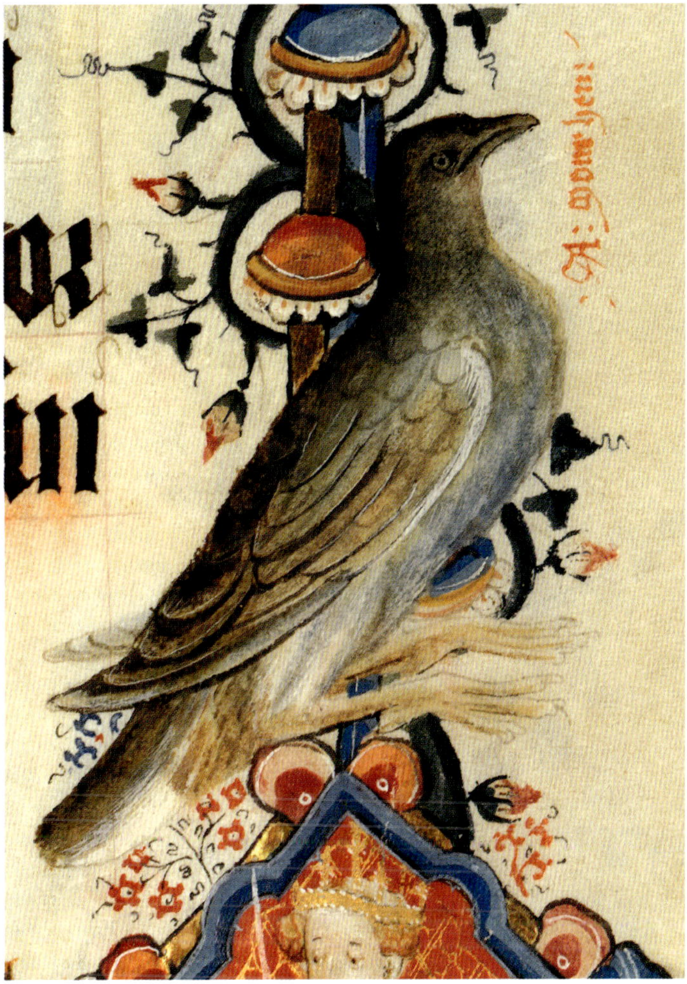

*7 A more hen: a moorhen, (p. 365, below). Enlargement on p. 11.*

reasonable number of pages should contain some decoration. It was to be symbolic of the importance and historical status of the community for which it was designed. The substance of each of its main sections did, however, dictate to a large extent the choice of subject matter and treatment. In the *Temporale* the chief festivals commemorate events chronicled in the New Testament. They are thus introduced by familiar scenes from the life of Christ, generally enclosed in large-scale initials and surrounded by elaborate marginal schemes in which associated narrative subjects, together with related images from the Old Testament, are prominently featured. Pages for many of the less important days of the liturgical year are given single illustrations representing the appropriate readings from the gospels, most of which come from the parables or miracle stories. In places where rich pictorial decoration might seem out of place, notably during the penitential season of Lent, a luxurious but more sober impression is achieved by the inclusion of shields of arms inside the main initials, their glowing heraldic colours lighting up the lines of text. On the most elaborate pages, marginal decoration is enhanced by the use of a mass of purely ornamental motifs, including tiny but lifelike birds. The Easter page (see frontispiece) contains no less than ten of these, several quite easily recognisable. This purely decorative use of bird figures is similar to work in other manuscripts of the period, especially those produced in France.

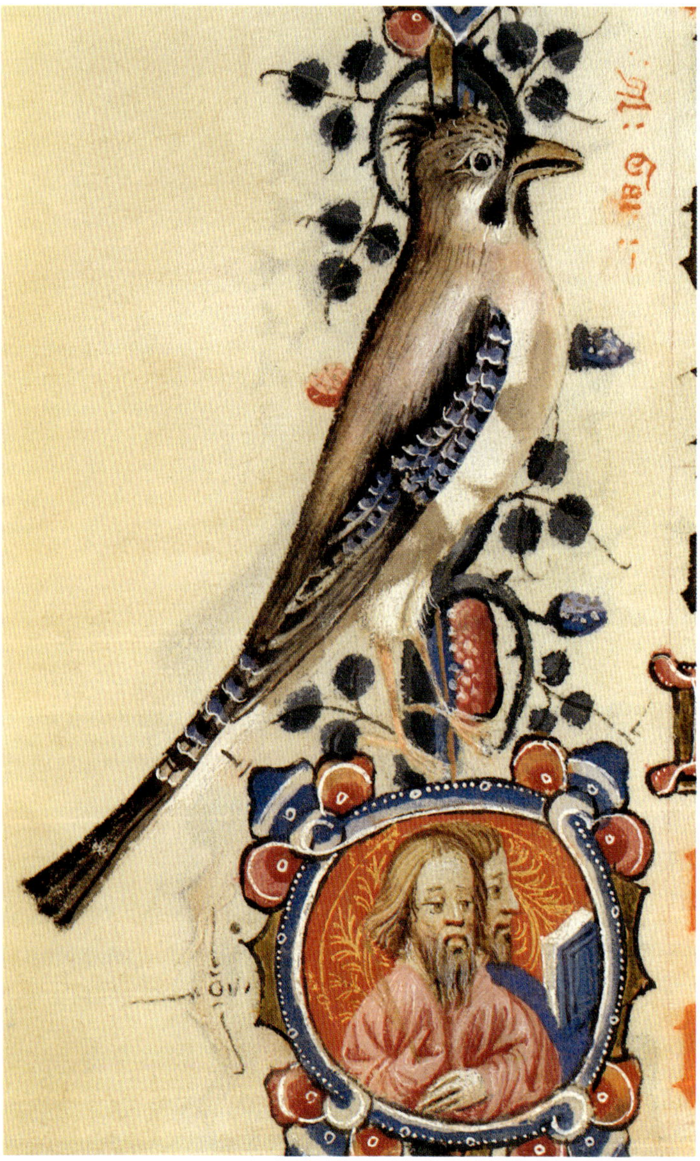

8 *A Gai: a jay,* (p. 366, *above*). *Enlargement on p. 12.*

The *Sanctorale* provides less scope for full-page decorative schemes, apart from those marking the feastdays of the Virgin Mary and of one or two other holy figures of universal or local importance, such as St Benedict. Each saint is represented within a 'portrait' initial, identified wherever possible by suitable attributes. Similarly the votive masses open with initials symbolising their individual intentions.

When Siferwas and his team came to devise a scheme of decoration for the central and most important section of the book, the text offered no clear thematic guidance, apart from the rather obvious device of filling its initials with images of the priest at the altar. On many pages this has in fact been done. Comprehensive decoration was, however, required for every page in this part of the book. Because the Missal was conceived as a tangible demonstration of Sherborne's standing, no doubt intended to be shown off to important visitors and potential patrons, a number of historical themes were therefore introduced.

From 705 until after the Conquest, when the bishop's seat was moved to Salisbury in 1075, Sherborne had been a bishopric. A sequence of images of the Saxon bishops, all duly named, is therefore included and there are a number of subtle reminders of the special relationship which still existed between the abbey and its contemporary bishop. Roundels in the lower margins enclose figures who display neatly written inscriptions relating to the early history of the church and to the foundation of the various religious orders, with due stress laid upon the supremacy of the Benedictines. Further into the section a similar series is devoted to the major benefactors of the abbey, most of them royal, who are shown holding up sealed charters detailing their gifts. Purely decorative material was required to fill the intervening spaces, especially in the lateral margins, and it is here, among the saints, the bishops and the kings, that the Sherborne birds, with their accompanying English names, are somewhat unexpectedly to be found.

These birds do not fly haphazardly around among the marginal foliage like their cousins on the Easter page. Instead, each one is carefully positioned within the framework enclosing the text of the page, in an arrangement not paralleled elsewhere except in Siferwas's other major manuscript, the Lovel Lectionary. Although badly damaged, the Lectionary does include two similarly placed birds, one of them a fragmentary spoonbill, though neither is identified by name.

The choice of birds and their positions on the pages of the Missal seem to follow no predetermined scheme. They are not drawn to a consistent scale, most noticeable in the case of the kingfisher (33), a naturally tiny bird which appears abnormally large by comparison with its neighbours. Apart from the fact that on each page the two selected birds appear respectively above and below the centre line, their placing is inconsistent. Some face inwards towards the text, some outwards to the edge of the page. Occasionally some attempt seems to have been made to achieve a symmetrical appearance on a double opening. The cormorant and the gannet (pp.368-9), the shelduck and the teal (pp. 370-1), the heron and

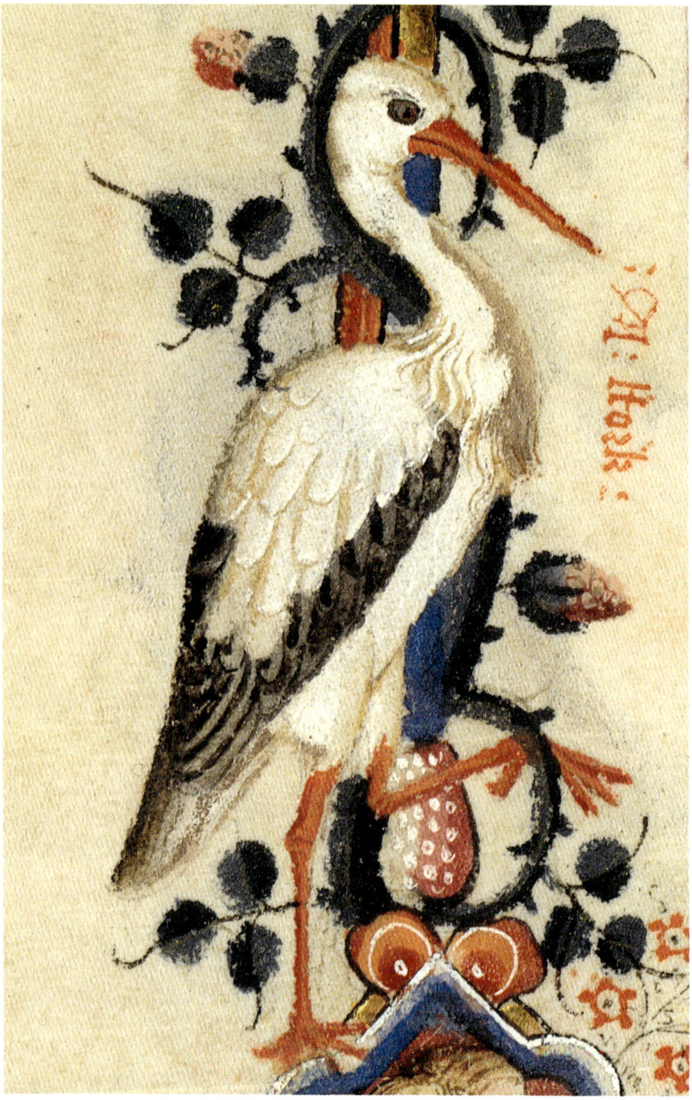

9 *A stork: a stork,* (p. 366, below).

the crane (pp. 386-7), and the barnacle goose and the wild goose (pp. 390-1) are all juxtaposed, though in each case only the lower part of the opening is involved. A greater degree of balance is achieved on pp. 374-5, where the peacock and the woodcock on the left are paired with the peahen and the quail on the right.

In only three places does the choice of bird appear to have any link to other material on the page. A goldfinch (5), unidentified but unmistakable, accompanies the sung preface for use at Epiphany (p. 364), where it adjoins a marginal roundel depicting the Magi following the star to Bethlehem. The star itself encloses a minute figure of the infant Christ. The goldfinch frequently appears in medieval Italian paintings of the Madonna and Child, its blood-red head foreshadowing Christ's Passion. The skylark (14), famous for soaring singing into the heavens, is similarly placed on p. 469, alongside a tiny vignette of the Ascension in which the prints of Christ's feet remain upon the rocks. Most relevant of all in the context of this particular book, the robin (32), identified as sharing the name of Robert with Sherborne's abbot, is carefully positioned on p. 382, alongside the *Communicantes* prayer in the canon of the mass, in which the principal early saints are named and commemorated. This is one of a number of places in the manuscript where a delicate compliment to the man behind the production of the Missal is quite clearly intended.

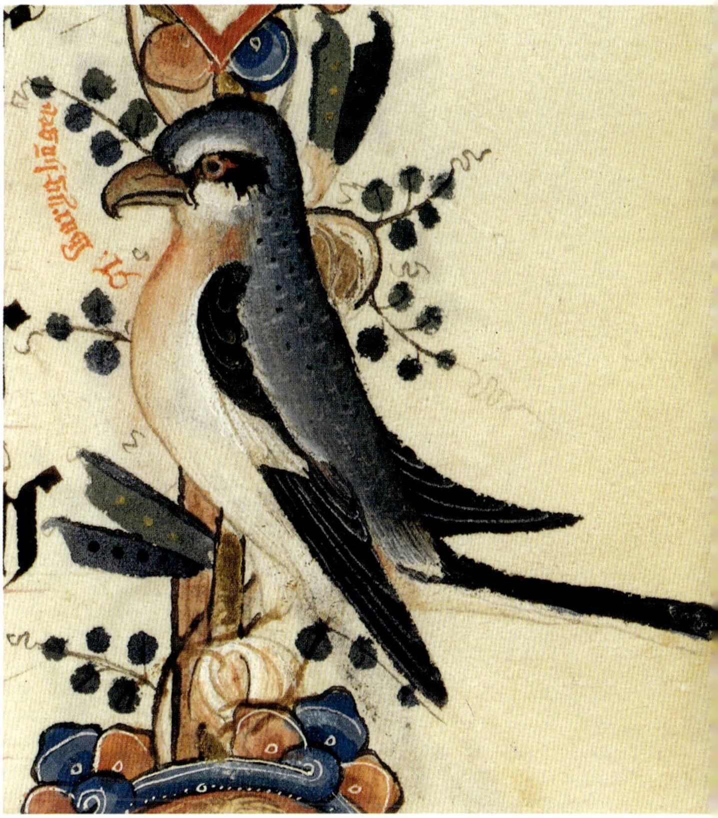

10 *A Waryghanger: a shrike, (p. 367, above).*

All the birds of the named series are to be found within some thirty pages in the central portion of the manuscript, though the sequence is interrupted where important elements, such as the Crucifixion miniature, intervene. Pictures 1, 30 and 51 provide examples of complete pages showing the overall arrangement.

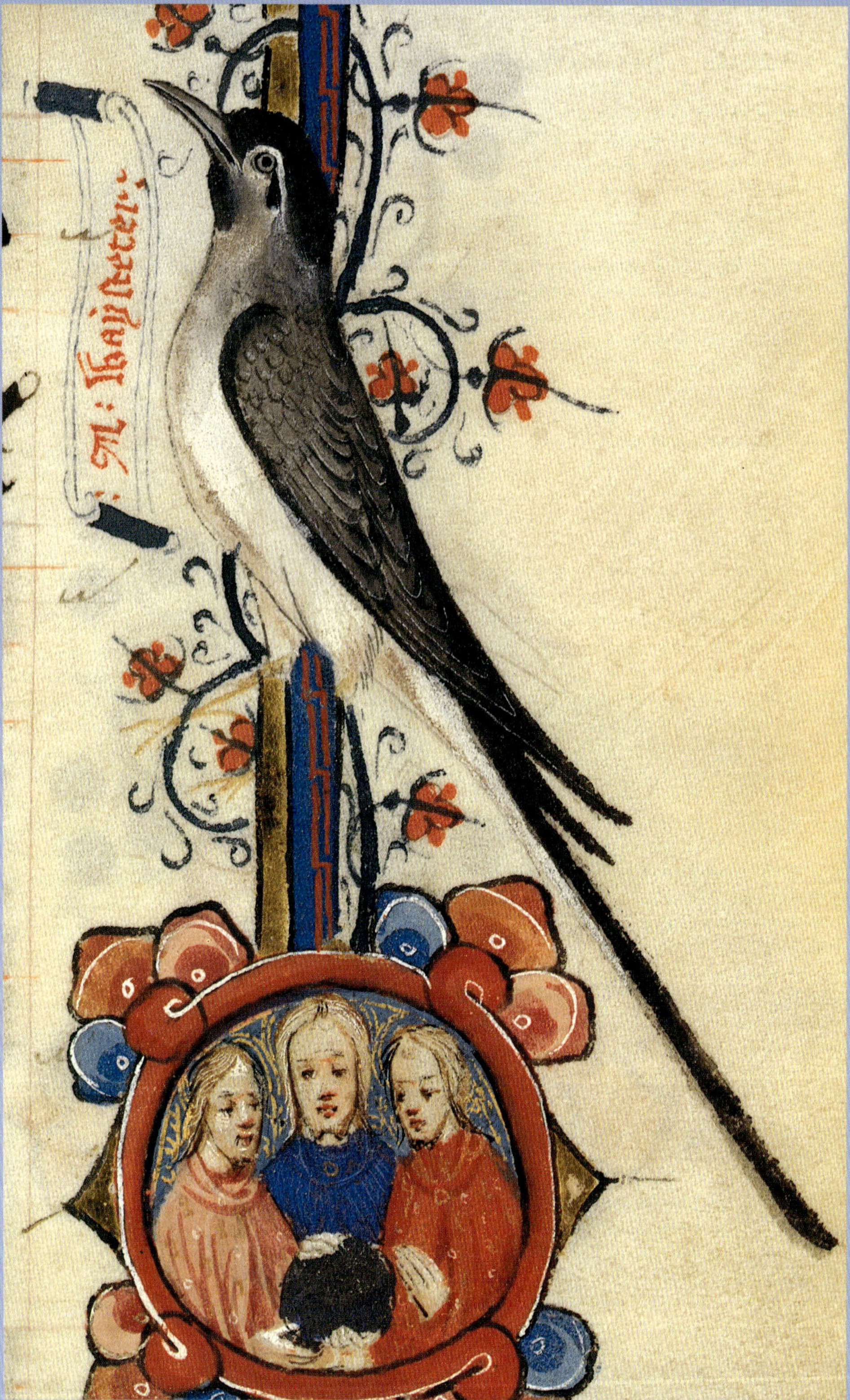

# THE NAMES OF THE BIRDS

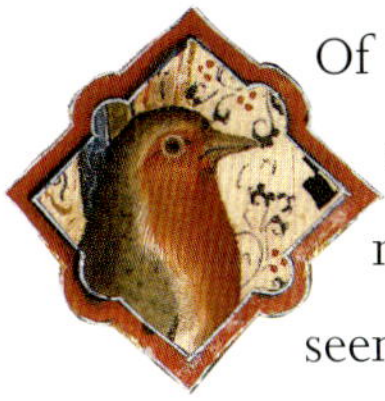

Of the forty-eight birds which appear in the margins of the central section of the Sherborne Missal, forty-one are accompanied by their names written in Middle English. These written names need first to be seen in relation to other marginal inscriptions in the manuscript. Mainly to be found on the major decorated pages of the *Temporale* and, apart from the bird names, in Latin, they offer an often very necessary gloss on the pictorial themes. Biblical references serve to explain and to articulate the different scenes brought together in such complicated programmes as those found on the Christmas and Easter pages. The frequent repetition of devotional phrases such as 'Gloria et honor deo' and

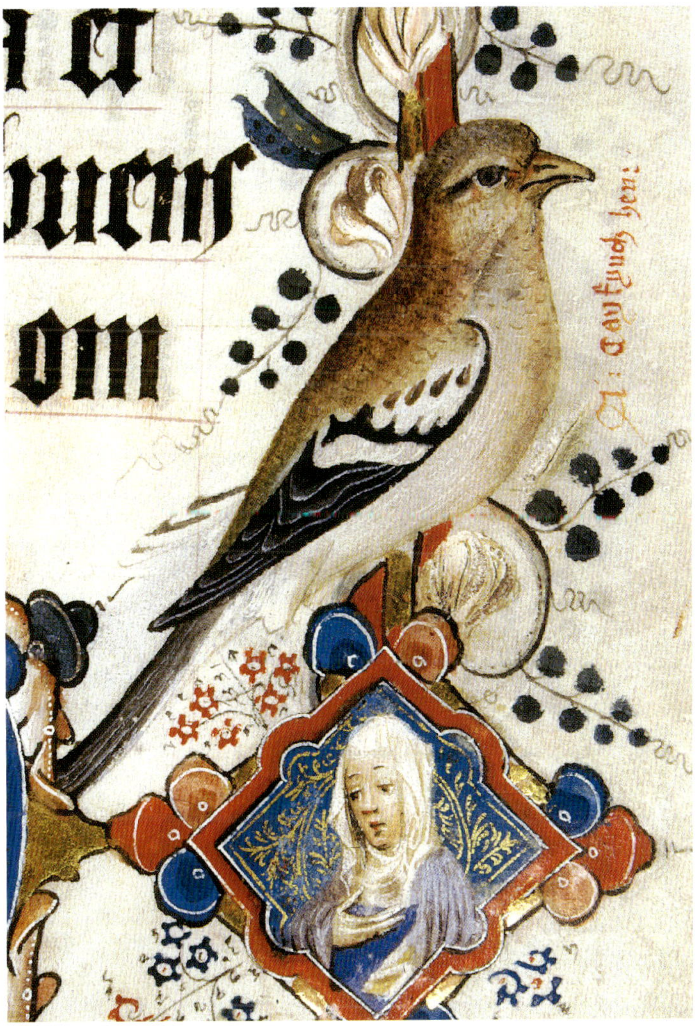

*11 A Cayfynch hen: a hen chaffinch,* *(p. 367, below).*

'Laus sit trinitati' helps, by association, to identify the bishop and the abbot when proper names are not supplied. These marginal inscriptions are placed on scrolls already built in to the overall design of each relevant page, often woven in and out of its framing bars and prepared by the application of a white-painted ground. Occasionally the scrolls remain blank, notably on the page devoted to the feast of the local St Wulsin (p. 397), where the complexities of the story perhaps proved as baffling to the 15th-century annotator as they do to the modern reader. Provision was even made for the inclusion of the names of the royal and noble persons whose coats of arms fill the initials for the season of Lent. All the inscriptions are written out in a not very sophisticated hand using a thin and apparently rather

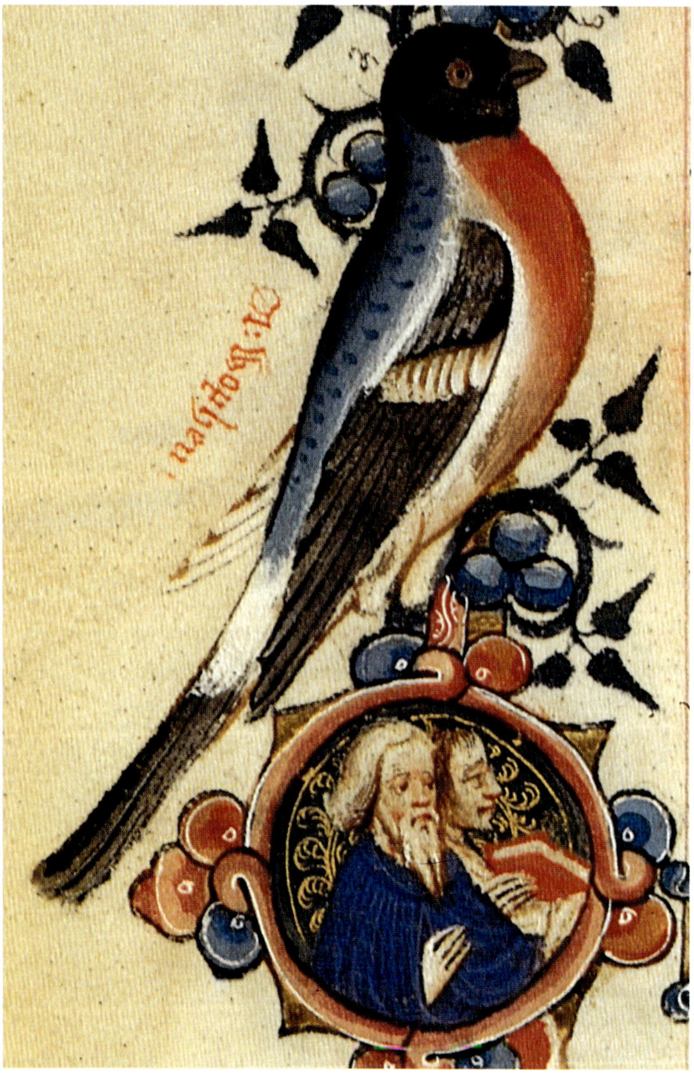

12 *A Wophen: a bullfinch, incorrectly described as a hen, (p. 368, above).*

scratchy nib. The small size of script required seems to have been very inhibiting to its scribe. The historical material in the lower margins of the central section of the book, though equally small, is much more confidently executed.

The bird names, though similar in character to the main body of inscriptions and certainly contemporary, were apparently not a part of the original page designs except in the case of the robin (32), which is named twice. One of these names, *rodduc robertus*, is given on a vertical scroll integrated into the marginal frame while the other, *roddok*, is written on a small scroll placed outside the frame itself. The possibility that this bird was regarded as a symbol of Sherborne's abbot has already been mentioned. As a series, the bird names, like the birds themselves, are not consistently positioned but appear to have been put in the nearest suitable space, sometimes inside and sometimes outside the frame. Nor are they consistent in appearance, although all but four are written in red ink as opposed to the black of the Latin inscriptions. Sixteen of them are unframed and the remainder are enclosed in simple scrolls, predominantly outlined in black but occasionally in red. The robin (32) and his companion the wren (31) are further distinguished by being named in blue inside their red scrolls. There is no way of establishing the relationship between the artist and the scribe. It is of course possible that they were one and the same, or that they were working closely

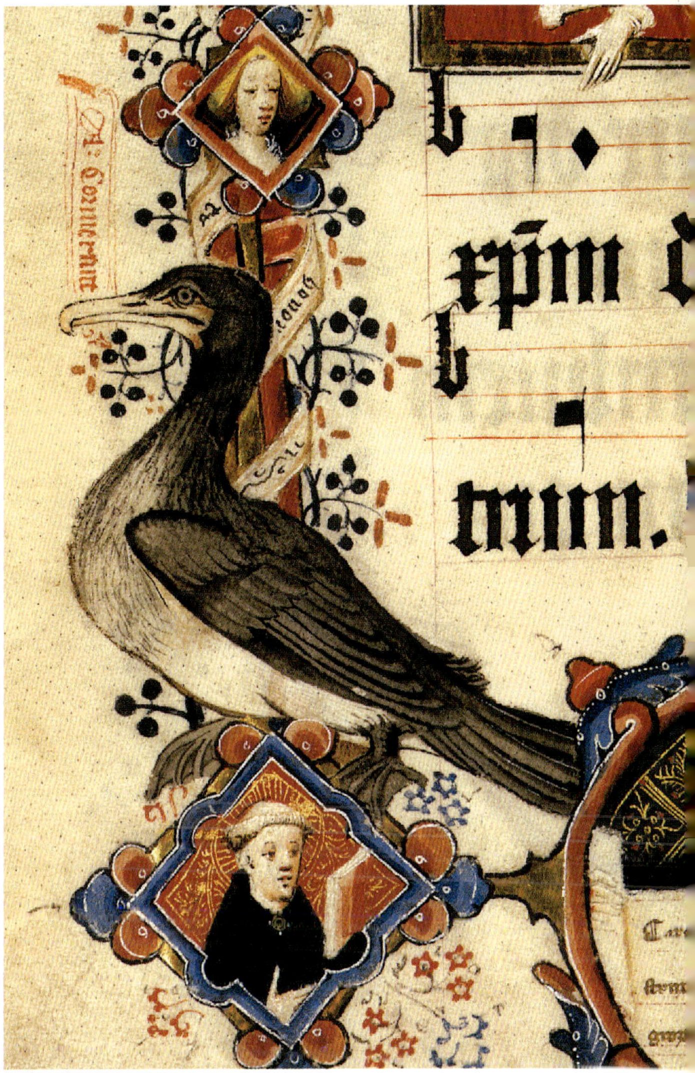

*13 A Cormerant: a cormorant (p. 368, below).*

together. It is also possible that the English names were supplied by someone who independently identified the birds from personal experience after the illumination had been finished.

Five of the names – *mose* (2, 3), *cayfynch* (11, 49), *wop* (12, 43), *tel* (19, 21) and *sparwe* (28, 29) – are duplicated to indicate, not necessarily accurately, both cock and hen birds of each species. The remaining thirty-one represent one of the most extensive single lists of vernacular bird names to have come down to us from the English Middle Ages, equal to that which can be extracted from Chaucer's *Parliament of Fowls*, written approximately twenty years before the production of the Missal. The two lists are, however, substantially different, with Chaucer's selection including in

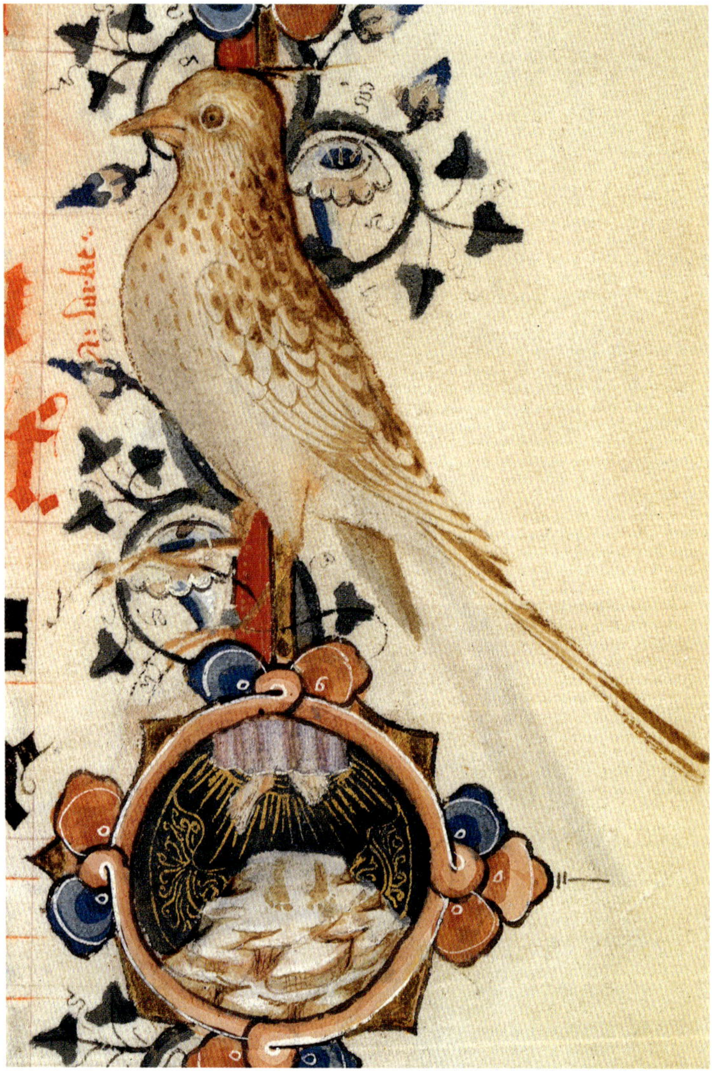

14 *A larke: a skylark,* (p. 369, *above*).

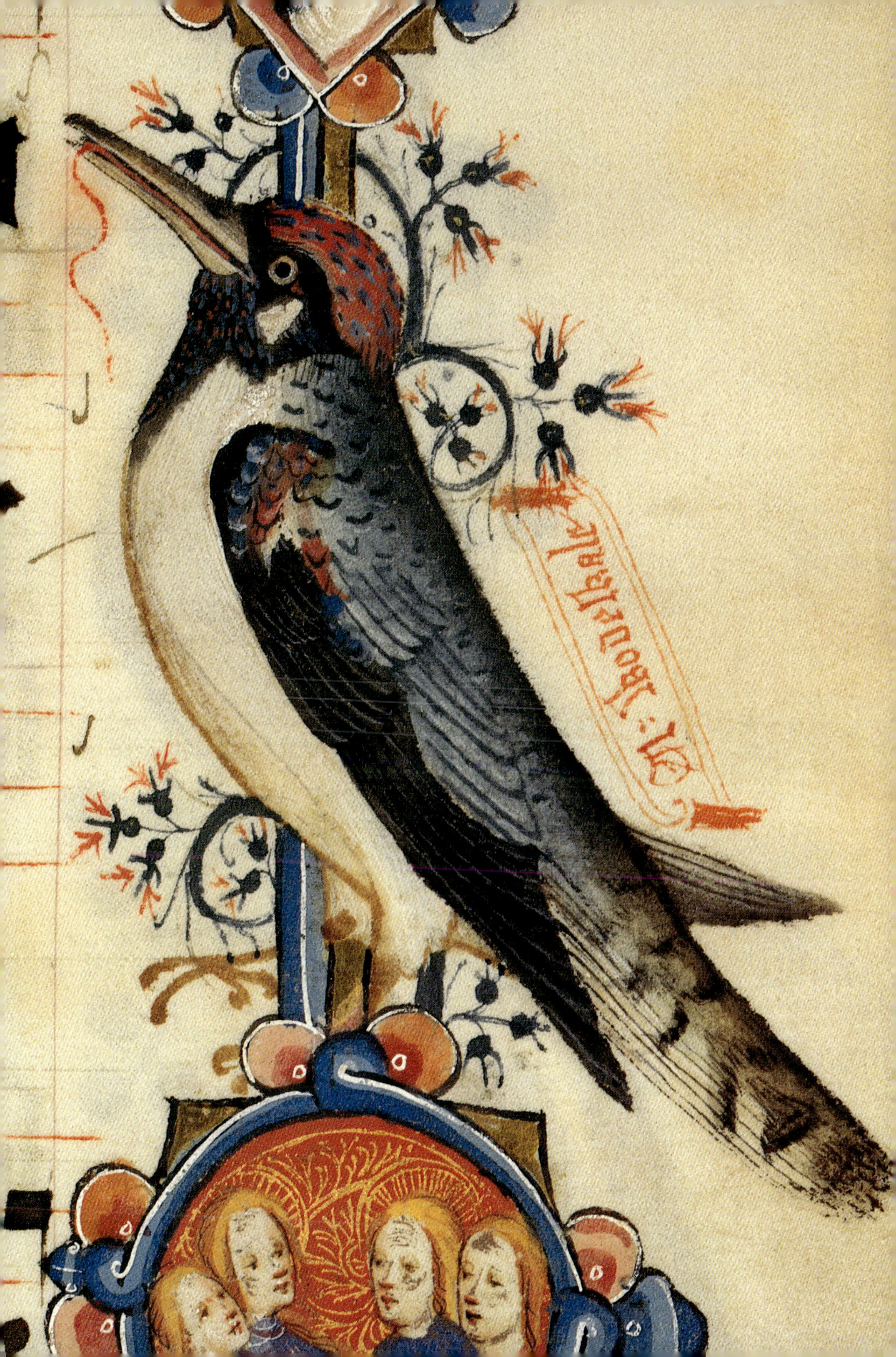
Wodewale

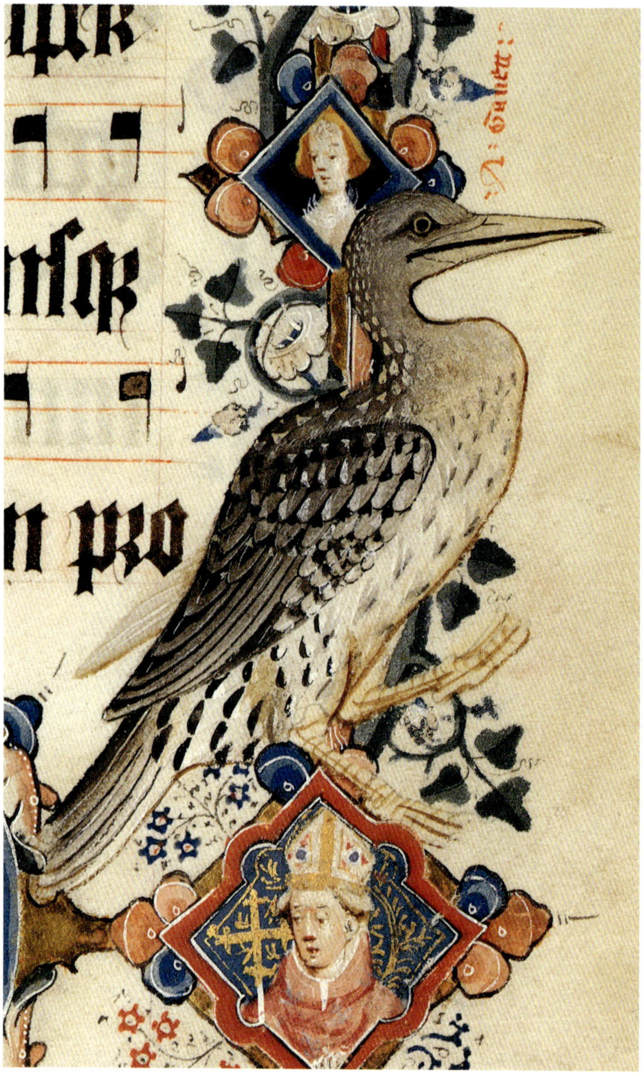

15 *A Ganett: a gannet,* (p. 369, *below*). *Enlargement on p.14*

particular a large number of native birds of prey, popularly used in the sport of hawking and therefore of special interest to his predominantly aristocratic audience. This class of bird is noticeably absent from the named series in the Missal, though one or two specimens are to be found among the purely decorative marginal birds. Although the Chaucer list has long been acknowledged as an important early source by historians of language engaged in the study of bird nomenclature, the complementary evidence of the Sherborne Missal has only recently been fully appreciated. Well known to historians of art ever since the publication of J.A. Herbert's monograph on the manuscript in 1920, where they are given in full, the bird names escaped the serious attentions of ornithologists

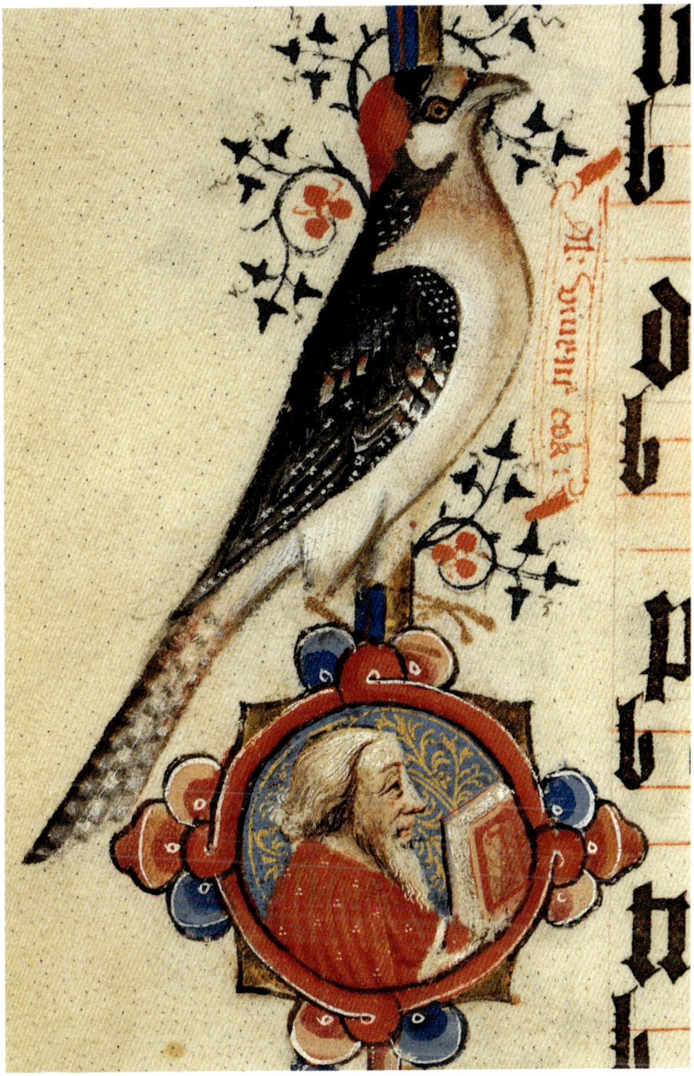

16 *A viuene (or possibly vinene) cok: a bird of uncertain species, possibly derived from a spotted woodpecker,* (p. 370, *above*).

and linguists alike until the early 1980s, when they were for the first time explored in some detail by Brunsdon Yapp in his work on the representation of birds in medieval manuscripts. His interest in the Missal had been aroused by Colonel E.D.V. Prendergast, then engaged in his own study of the local birds of Dorset. Yapp's work has now, in its turn, led to the incorporation of the Sherborne material in the revised edition of W.B. Lockwood's dictionary of British bird names, published as recently as 1993, from which much of the following information is taken. Readers should bear in mind the importance of oral transmission in the survival of vernacular material of this kind, a substantial part of which goes back to Anglo-Saxon times.

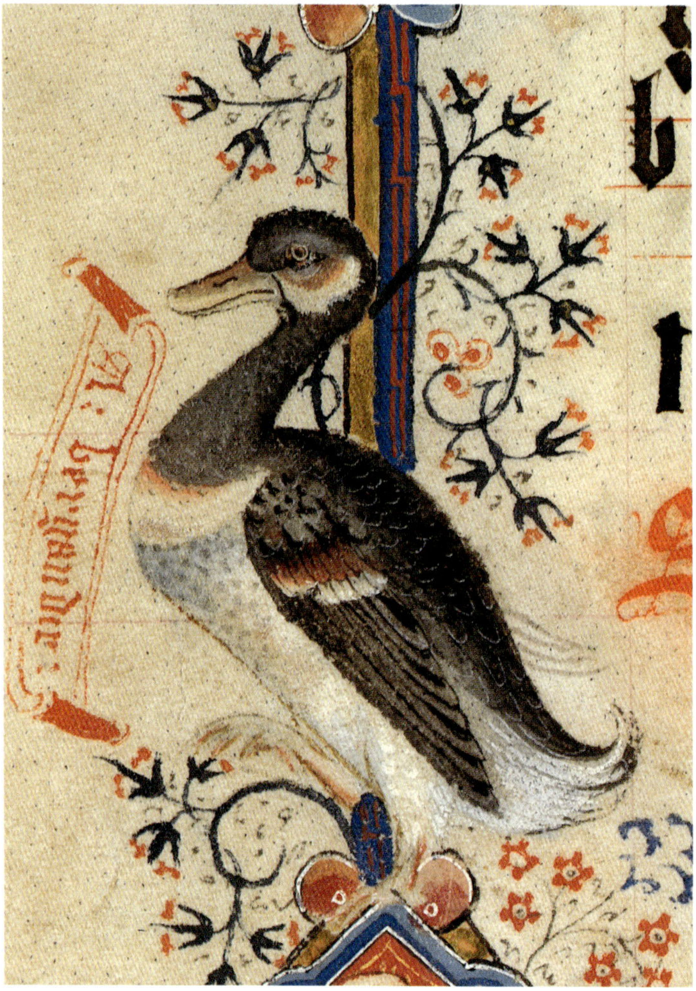

17 *A bergandir: a shelduck,* (p. 370, below).

A high proportion of the Sherborne Missal bird names can readily be equated with names in familiar modern use, particularly if they are read aloud. Little difficulty will be encountered with *more hen* (7), *gai* (8), *stork* (9), *cayfynch* (11, 49), *cormerant* (13), *larke* (14), *ganett* (15), *tel* (19, 21), *pohen* (26), *qayle* (27), *sparwe* (28, 29), *wrenne* (31), *morcoc* (34), *grenefynch* (35), *throstil* (37), *stare* (38), *heyrun* (40), *fesaunt* (41), *linet* (45) or *goos* (46). Both medieval and modern forms are given in the captions to the illustrations. In one or two cases, notably *throstil* (37), the medieval name is applied to a bird other than that with which it might be associated today.

Some of the names, both simple and complex, require additional comment. Several species in the manuscript are designated *mose*, either in its simple form (2, 3)

18 *A Waysteter: a wagtail, (p. 371, above). Enlargement on p. 22.*

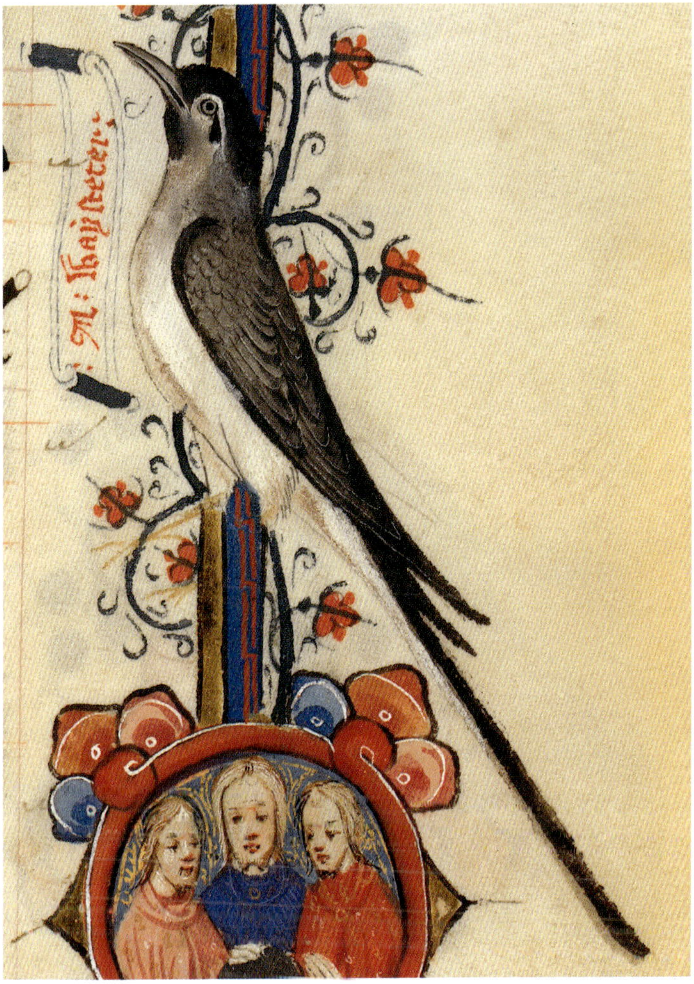

or in combination with a qualifying adjective as in *col mose* (6) or *tayl mose* (39). By the later Middle Ages this was more usually expanded to *titmose* (titmouse), which has in its turn been abbreviated to provide the *tit* of the present day. Here *mose* alone seems to indicate the blue tit or great tit. *Col mose* is appropriate to any of the family marked out by dark plumage on the head. *Tayl mose* is thought to be unique to the Missal and clearly indicates a long-tailed titmouse.

The designation *wop* (12, 43) for bullfinch appears to be a variant of *mwope*, recorded in Dorset dialect and paralleled in north-west England as *mawp*. *Scnite* (23) is an alternative spelling for *snite*, an ancient name for snipe, long used locally in the south-west of England. *Mew* (48), today exclusively a literary term, was the native English name for seagull from before the Conquest until well into the 17th century.

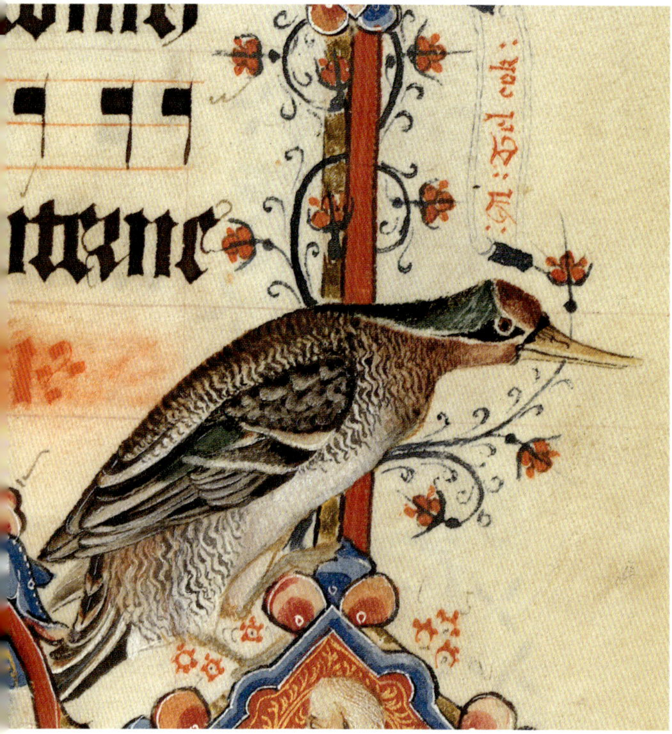

19 *A Tel cok: a male teal, (p. 371, below).*

One of the more complex names offered by the Missal is *waryghanger* (10), a variant of *wariangle*, an ancient name for the shrike or butcher-bird. Local versions of this name have been found in several areas of England, notably in the midlands and the north. Lockwood suggests that this specific form, found only in the Missal, may have been influenced by another local bird name, *withyhanger*, the Dorset dialect name for tree-creeper. Another name of special interest is *bergandir* (17), a common name for shelduck found as far apart as Northumberland and the Isle of Wight. This is however an exceptionally early record of its use. The Missal is also the earliest source for the use of *waysteter* (18), or wagstart, as an identification for the wagtail, deriving from the Old English *steort* for tail.

*Wodewale* (22) is equivalent to *woodwall*, used locally in Somerset for the green woodpecker and in Hampshire for the spotted. However, there are earlier sources where this term is applied to the golden oriole, now only rarely seen in England. The colourful character of both species may have inspired the transfer of the name. The *kyngynsfystere* (33) is readily identifiable with the modern kingfisher, but the Missal is nonetheless the first source in which it is found used specifically as the name of a bird. Earlier instances show it as a personal name or nickname. The goose identified as a *bornet* (44) might in medieval terms be either a barnacle or a brent goose, as the two were not distinguished as separate species. The Sherborne specimen clearly represents the former. *Vuelduare* (47) is one of many variant spellings for fieldfare, recorded in Wiltshire as *velverd* and elsewhere in the south-west as *veldiver*. Chaucer called this bird the 'frosty feldefare', reflecting its character as a winter visitor to pastureland.

A number of the more esoteric Middle English bird names recorded in the Missal can thus be related to more recent local usage, surviving into modern times in the spoken language of areas geographically close to the Dorset abbey for which the manuscript was created. This supports the idea that the birds may have been labelled as an afterthought by a specifically local hand. One bird above all offers more than one reflection of local interest. Both *roddok* (in the outer margin) and *rodduc* (within the frame) are offered as names for the robin (32). These names and their variants were widely used from Anglo-Saxon times until the 19th century, today's familiar 'robin' gaining currency no earlier than the 16th century. *Reddock* is a known Dorset form. However, the robin of the Missal is also designated *robertus*, the name of which 'robin' is a diminutive. The name Robert is said to come from the Germanic terms for 'bright fame' but may also have been associated with the Latin *ruber* (red), suited to a redbreasted bird. It does not now seem possible to establish whether this name was in common use for the robin as early as the beginning of the 15th century. What does seem certain is that the bird was here used in oblique compliment to Sherborne's abbot, Robert Brunyng, chief architect of the production of the manuscript, giving at least one of the marginal bird studies a function beyond the purely ornamental.

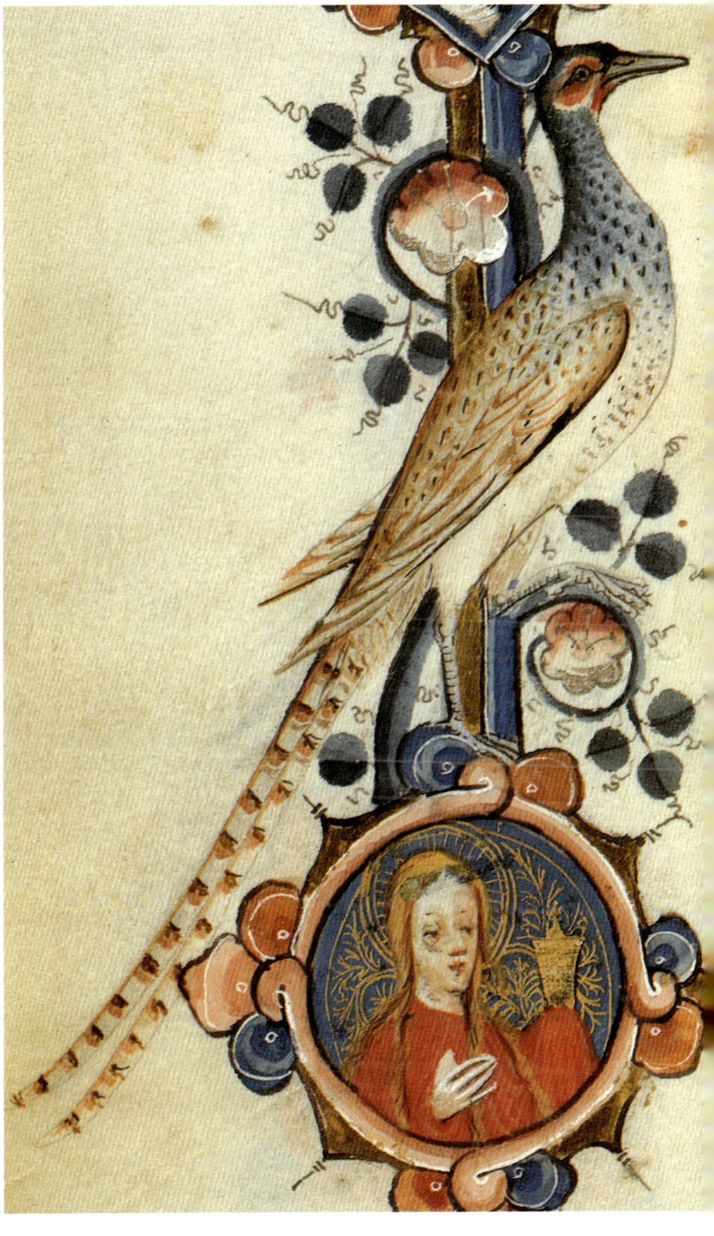

20 *Unidentified bird: a cock pheasant, (p. 372, above).*

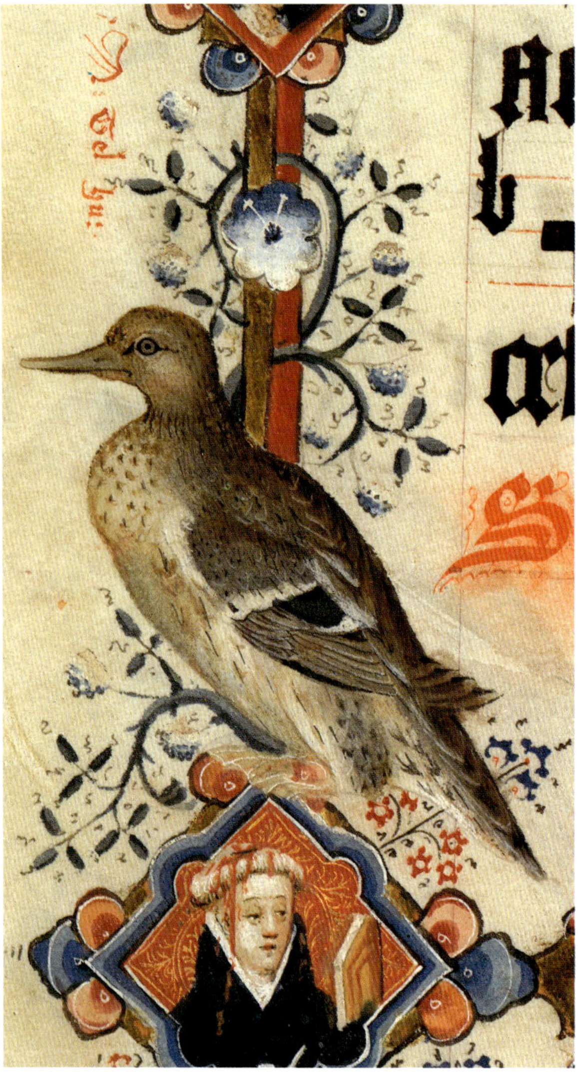

21 *A Tel hn: a female teal*, (p. 372, *below*).

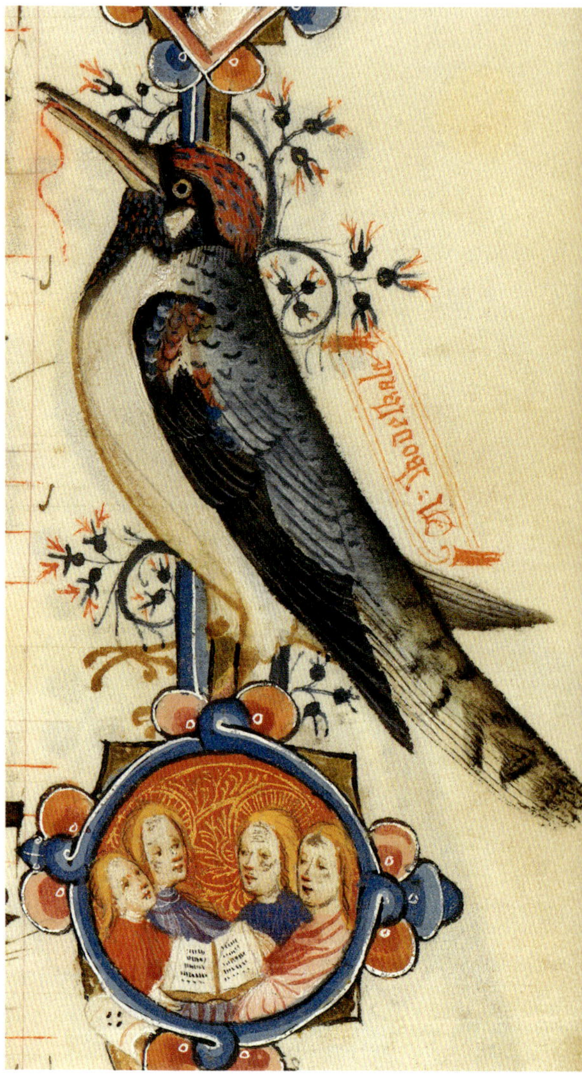

22 *A wodewale: a woodpecker, also shown on* p. 27, (p. 373, *above*).

Two of the English names, *viuene* (or possibly *vinene*) *cok* (16) and *fyne hen* (36), have yet to be identified with a specific bird. Although the two birds in question are portrayed as very different in shape, much of their colouring is similar, particularly about the heads and tails. Overall the latter is not unlike a lesser spotted woodpecker. The term *fina* has been cited by some linguists as an early name for woodpecker, apparently found in an Anglo-Saxon vocabulary, but no later medieval example of the word has yet come to light.

Seven birds in the marginal series are not named at all, though only one (4) seems truly unidentifiable. Crested and burdened with a heavy bill, it appears at

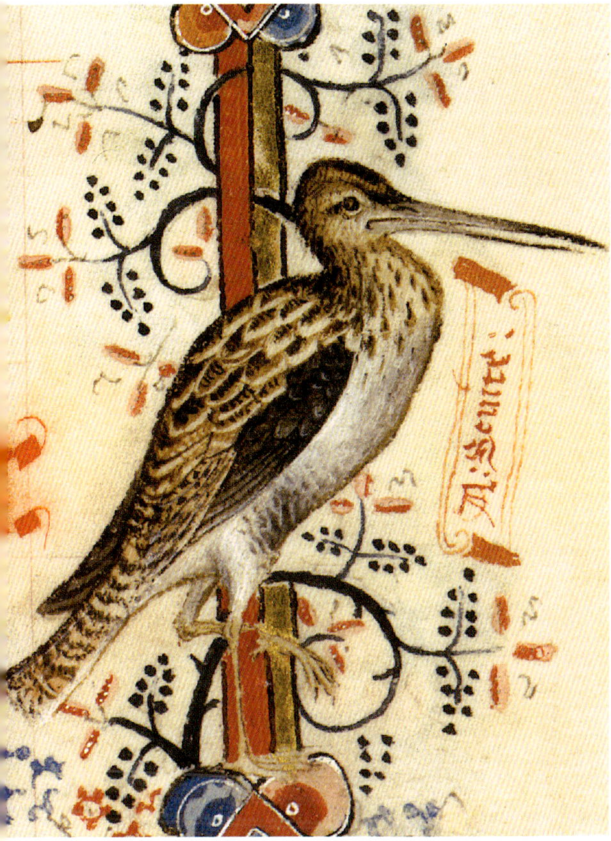

23 *A Scnite*: *a snipe*, (p. 373, below).

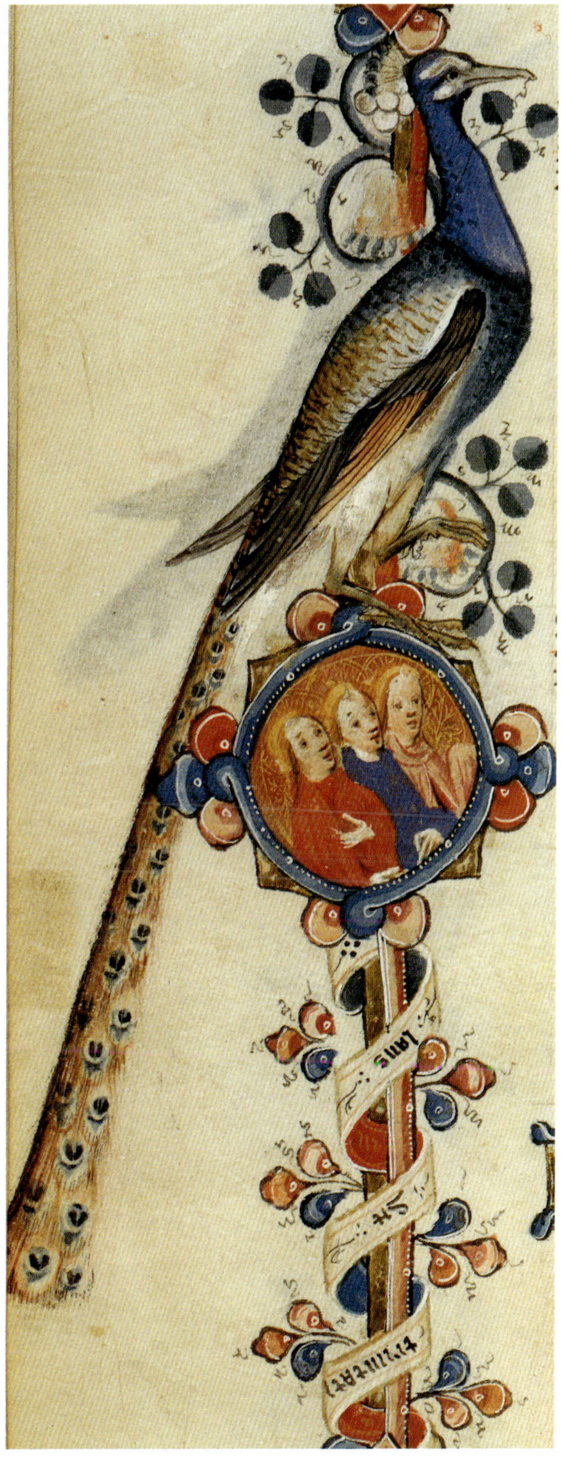

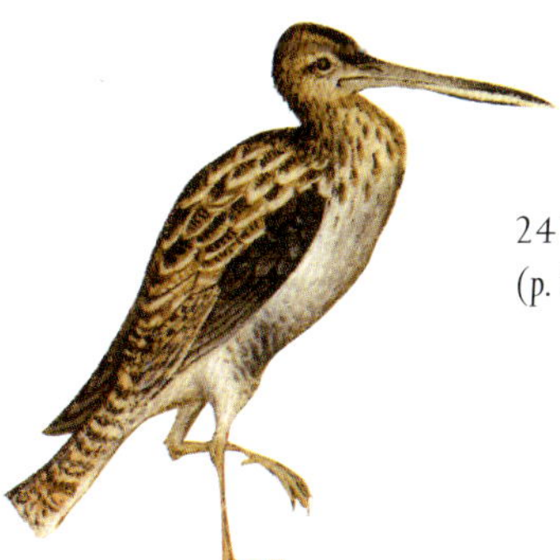

24 Unidentified bird: *a peacock*, (p. 374, *above*).

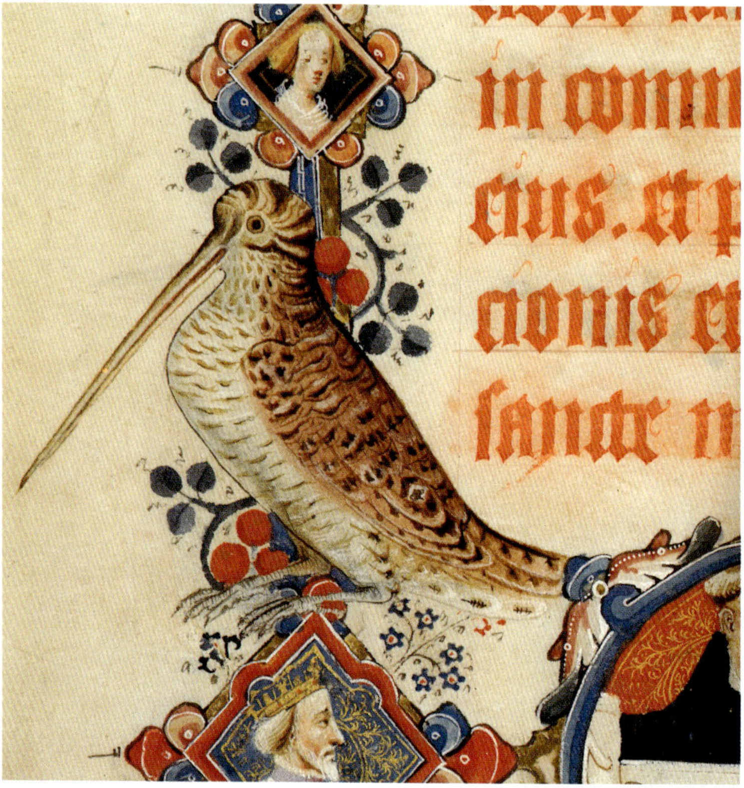

25 Unidentified bird: *a woodcock*, (p. 374, below).

first glance to display a blend of characteristics drawn from the shrike (10) and the jay (8). The lower bird on the same page (5), also unnamed, is readily recognisable as a goldfinch by its distinctive and colourful plumage and shown again later in the series (35), where it is erroneously called *grenefynch*. The cock pheasant (20) and the peacock (24), though their naturally rich colouring is perhaps a little muted, are beautifully depicted but unlabelled, though the hen bird of each (41 and 26 respectively) is identified. Both appear in a purely decorative context elsewhere in the manuscript (see page 60). One of the three remaining birds, the crane (42), also reappears among the decorative features. The second (50), posed on one leg while it swallows an eel, is probably a heron, though not quite so convincingly coloured as the specimen already included (40). The third (25) is a remarkably accurate drawing of a woodcock, perhaps unknown to the hand writing the English names but possibly overlooked because it shares a page with the equally anonymous peacock.

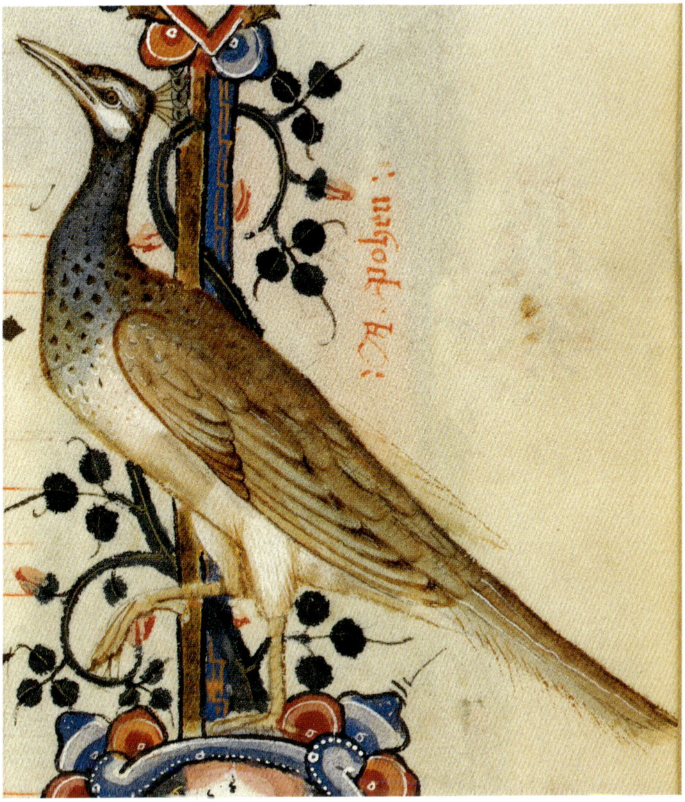


26 *A Pohen: a peahen*, (p. 375, above).

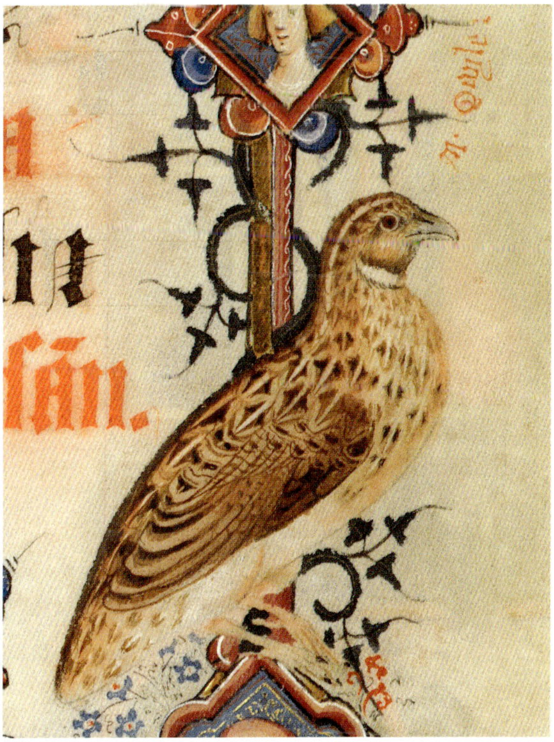


27 *A Qayle: a quail*, (p. 375, below).

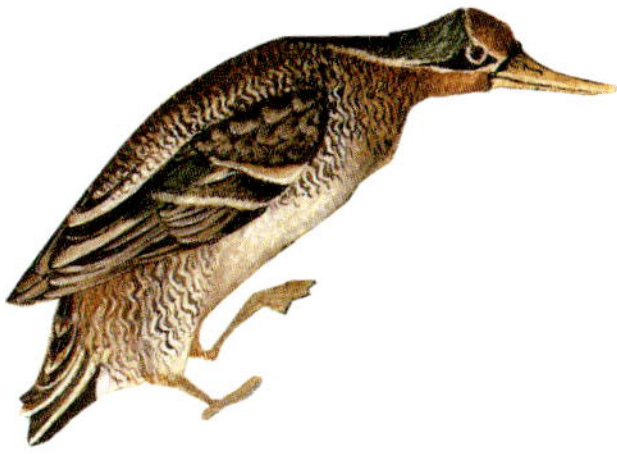

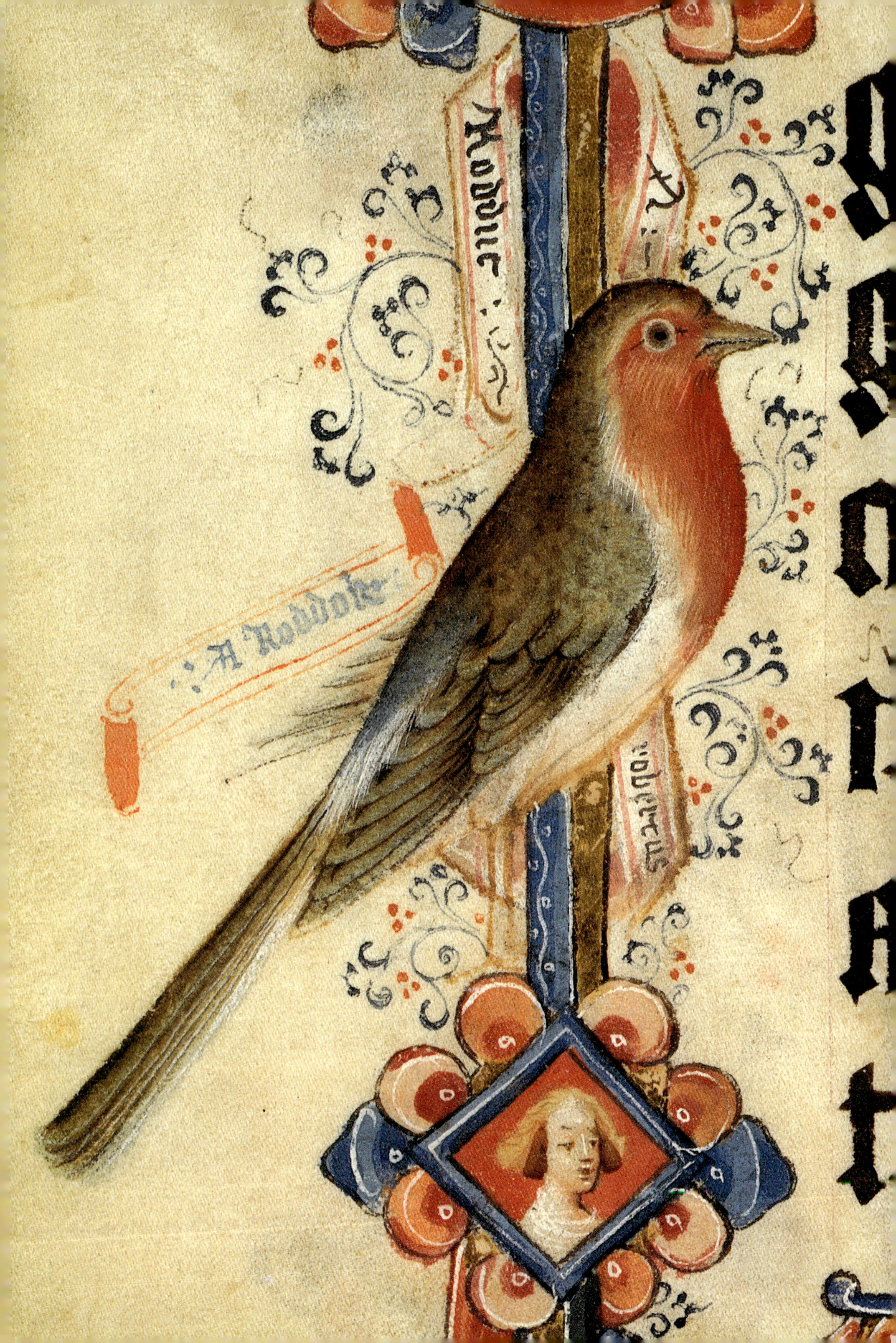
Rodduc
A Roddoke
robertus

29 *A Sparwe cok*: a male house sparrow, (p. 377, below).

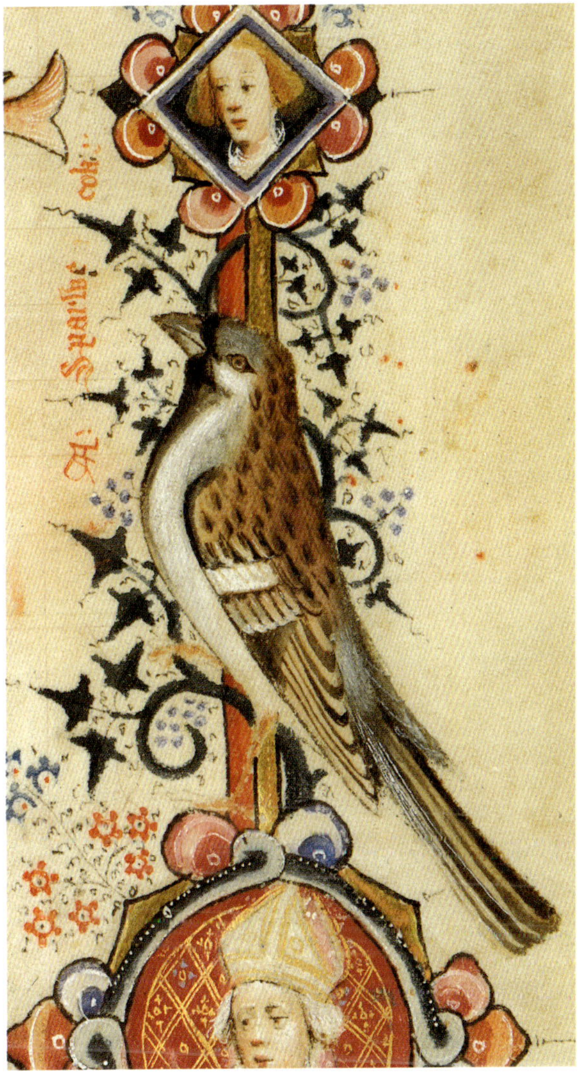


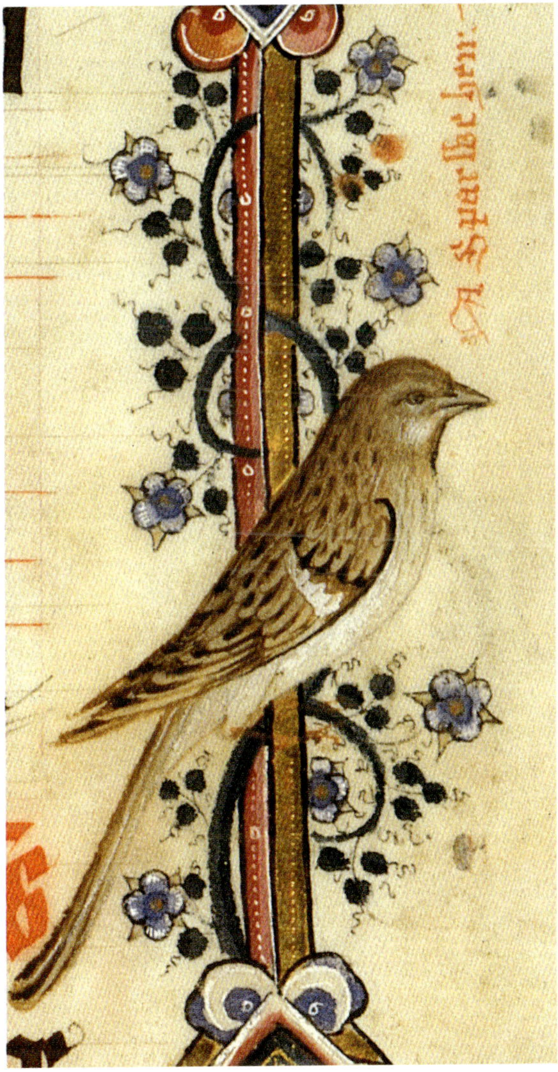


28 *A Sparwe hen*: a female house sparrow, (p. 377, above).

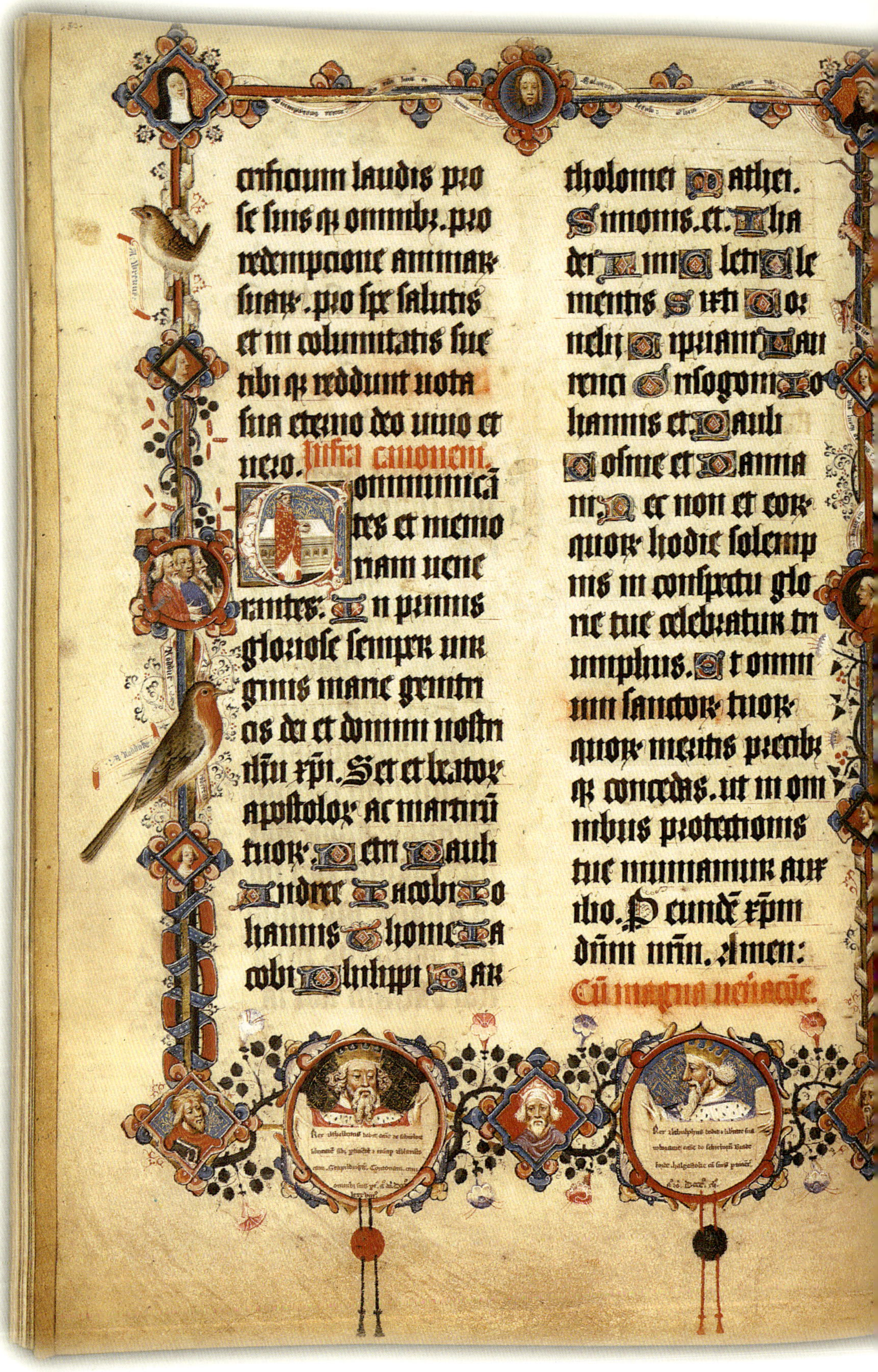
canticum laudis pro
se suisque omnibus: pro
redempcione animarum
suarum: pro spe salutis
et incolumitatis sue
tibique reddunt vota
sua eterno deo vivo et
vero. Infra canonem.
Communican-
tes et memo-
riam vene-
rantes: In primis
gloriose semper vir-
ginis marie genitri-
cis dei et domini nostri
ihesu christi. Set et beatorum
apostolorum ac martirum
tuorum: Petri Pauli
Andree Iacobi Io-
hannis Thome Ia-
cobi Philippi Bar-
tholomei Mathei.
Simonis. et Tha-
dei. Lini Cleti Cle-
mentis Sixti Cor-
nelii Cypriani Lau-
rencii Grisogoni Io-
hannis et Pauli
Cosme et Damia-
ni.
quorum hodie solemp
nis in conspectu glo
rie tue celebratur tri
umphus. Et omni
um sanctorum tuorum
quorum meritis precibus
que concedas. ut in om
nibus protectionis
tue muniamur auxi
lio. Per eundem christum
dominum nostrum. Amen:
Cum magna veneracione.

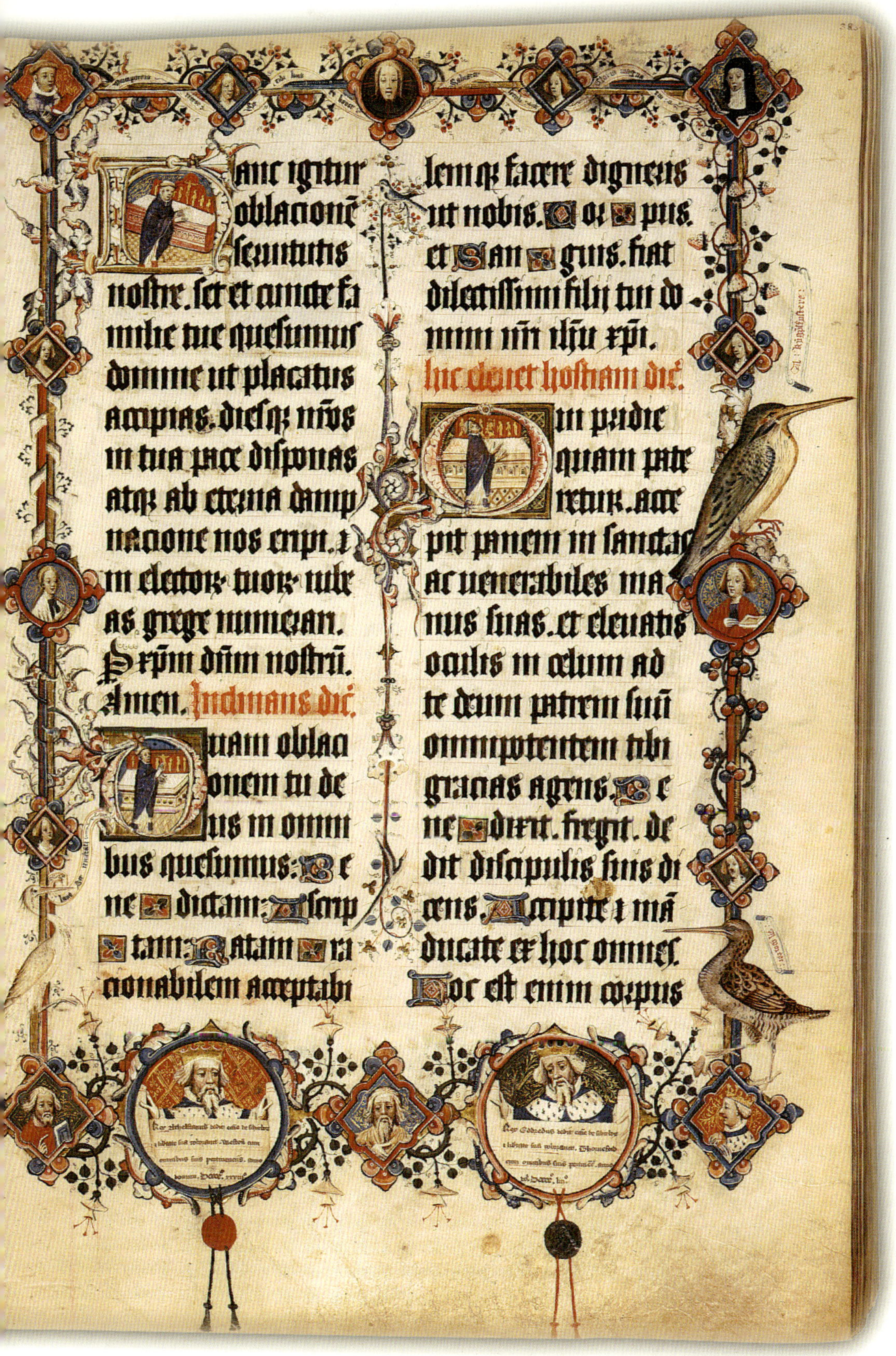

30 *An opening from the manuscript, with decoration including royal benefactors of Sherborne holding sealed charters. The marginal birds are identified as wren, robin, kingfisher and moorcock, (pp. 382–3).*

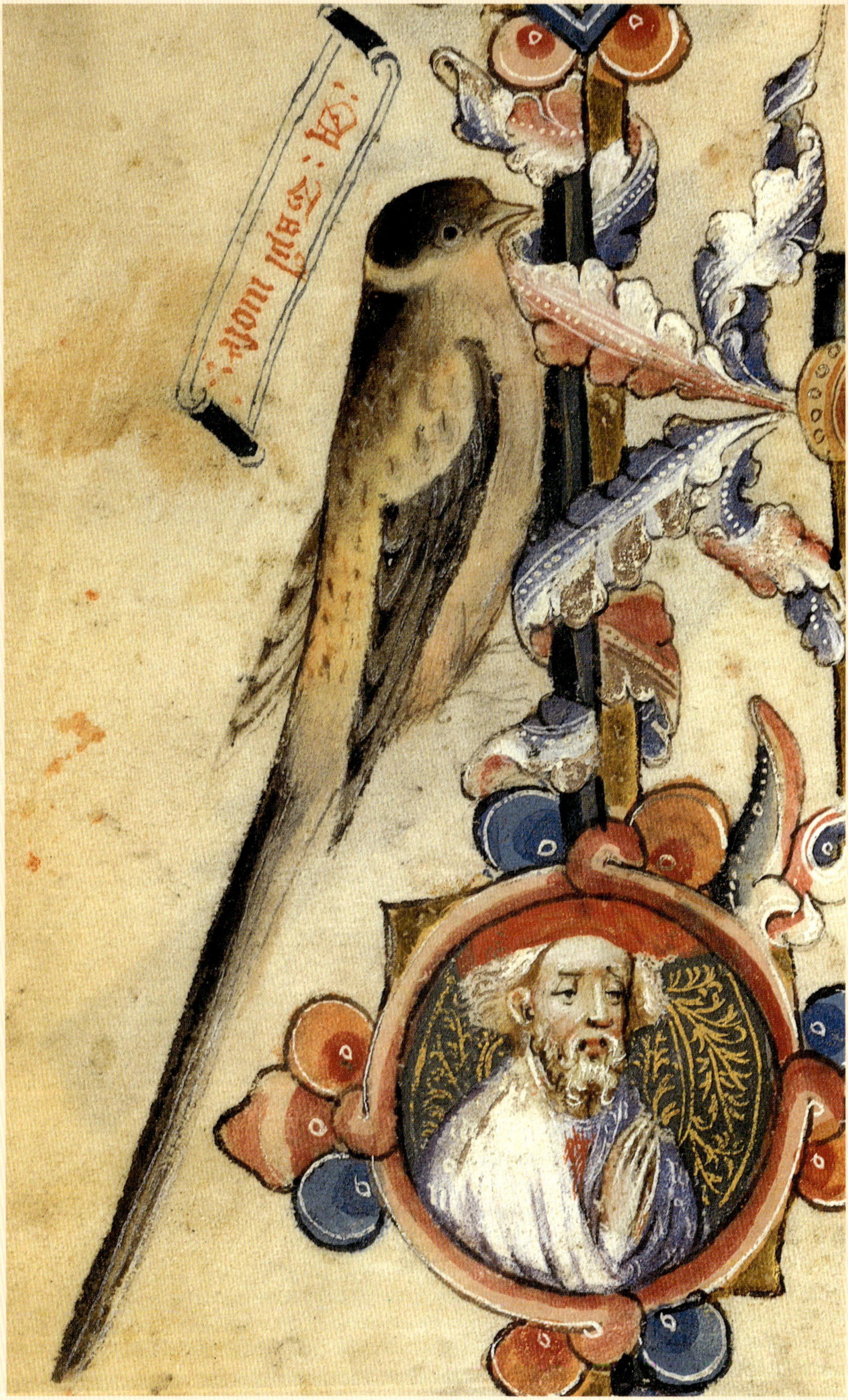

# THE PORTRAYAL OF THE BIRDS

The majority of the bird images in the Sherborne Missal are certainly intended to be recognisable, reflecting the chief characteristics of their various species, though they cannot of course be regarded as scientific studies in any modern sense. As noted above, only one (4) seems to be totally unidentifiable, while two more (16, 36) are obscure though possibly intended as cock and hen of a single type. It should not be forgotten that all hand-drawn representations of natural subjects inevitably take on some flavour of the artistic style of the age which produced them. This is clearly reflected in portraits of human subjects. Anyone studying historic surveys of British birds will quickly come to distinguish between illustrations published in different centuries, however carefully observed they may be. Some of the birds in the Missal are remarkable for the accuracy of their detail, others are much less convincing, relying on a general

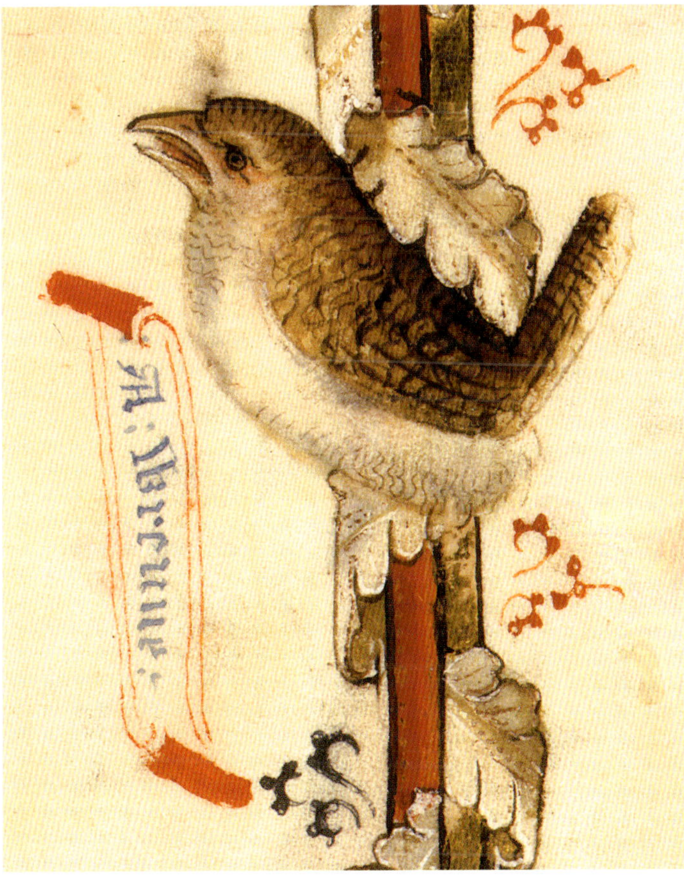


31 *A wrenne: a wren,*
(p. 382, *above*).

impression or even a single characteristic to convey identity. Colour is of fundamental importance in many cases. Indeed, in the portrayal of the tiny birds used for purely decorative purposes, it is often the most vital clue (see frontispiece). Readers will form their own opinions about the accuracy of the Sherborne bird images in the light of their own preferred sources for comparison.

There is little to indicate how the bird artist set about producing his figures. It is almost certainly fair to assume that the birds as we see them in the Missal were based upon a collection of models or sketches owned by or directly accessible to the illuminator. They can hardly have been drawn for the first time upon these elaborate, expensive and carefully finished pages. Evidence of the model books used by medieval artists in any medium is scanty. The books themselves were working tools

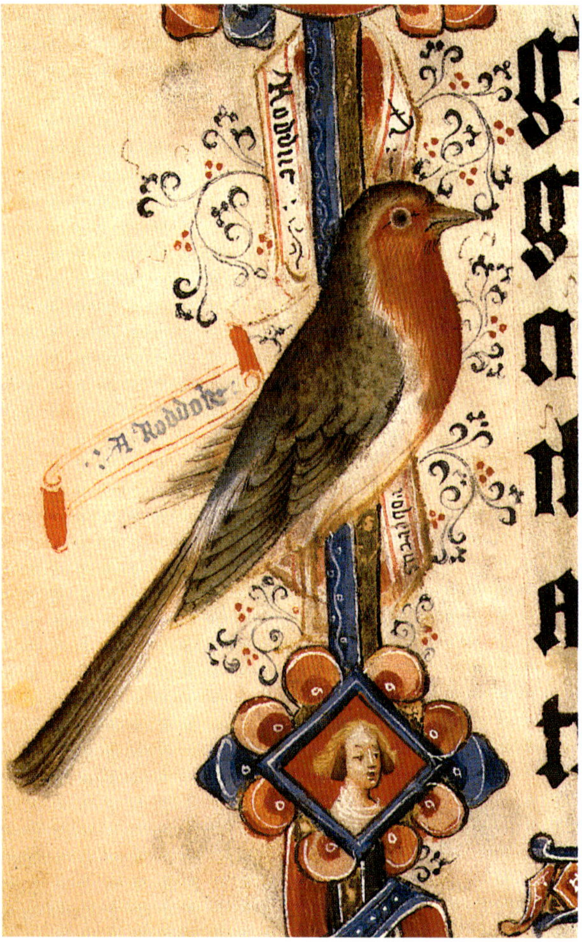


*32 A Roddok (also Rodduc robertus): a robin, (p. 382, below). Enlargement on p. 38.*

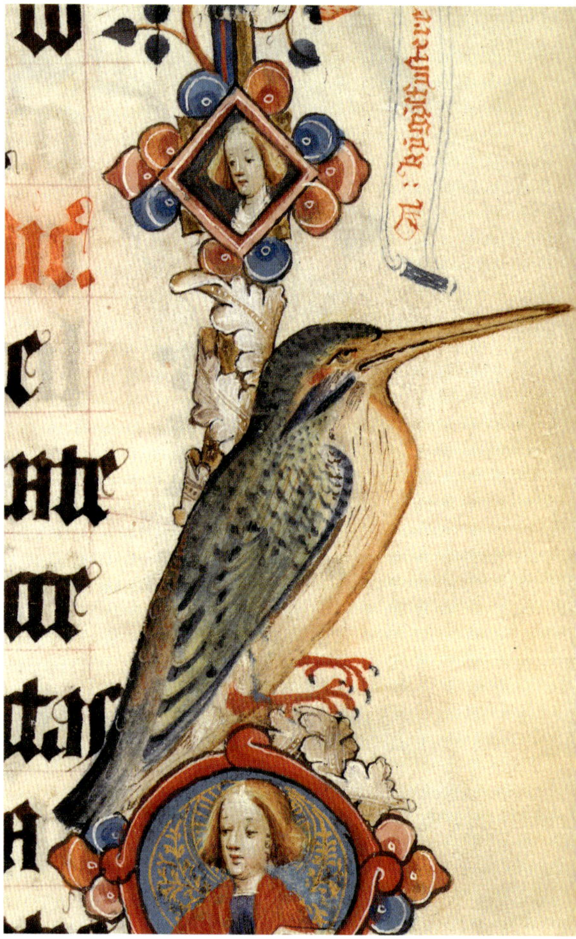

*33 A kyngynsfystere: a kingfisher, (p. 383, above).*

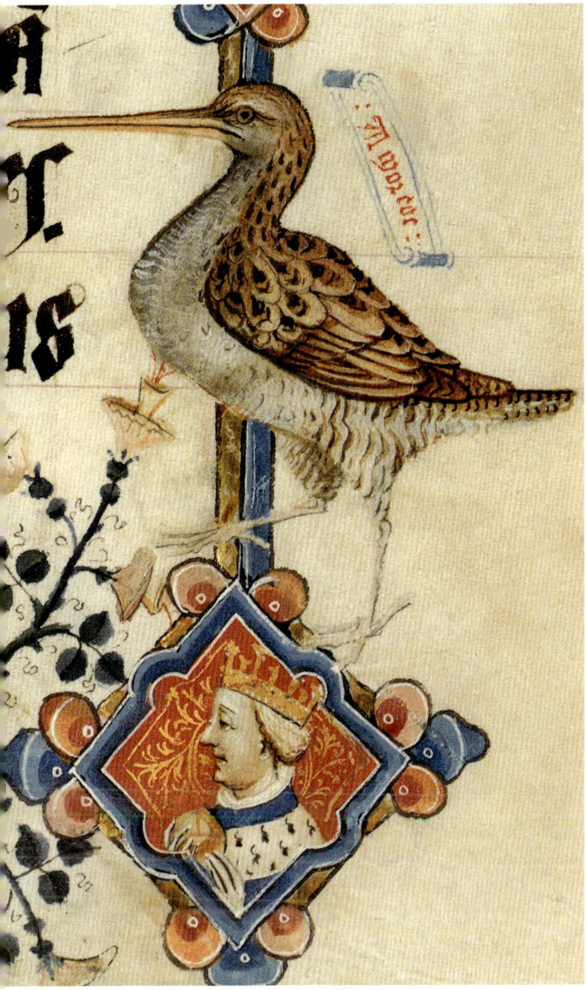

34 *A morcoc: possibly intended for a godwit, (p. 383, below).*

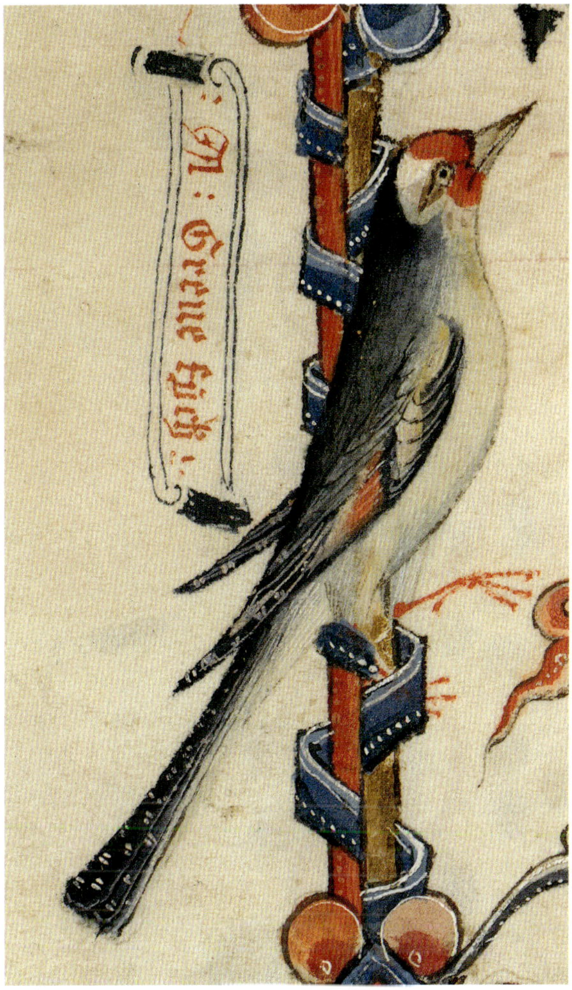


35 *A Grene fynch: a misidentified goldfinch, (p. 384, above).*

and as such vulnerable to wear and tear, discarded when too soiled for further use.

Only two late medieval English pattern books of any kind have survived, one devoted largely to initial letters. However, the other, once the property of the 17th-century diarist, Samuel Pepys, and now preserved with his personal library at Magdalene College, Cambridge, does include four leaves of bird studies, several of which are labelled with English names in a late medieval hand. A date around 1400 has been proposed for these pages and they have inevitably found themselves linked to the Sherborne Missal's artist, though they in fact bear very little stylistic resemblance to his work. The Sherborne birds have also been compared with a body of bird studies produced in northern Italy during the late 14th century, notably in the

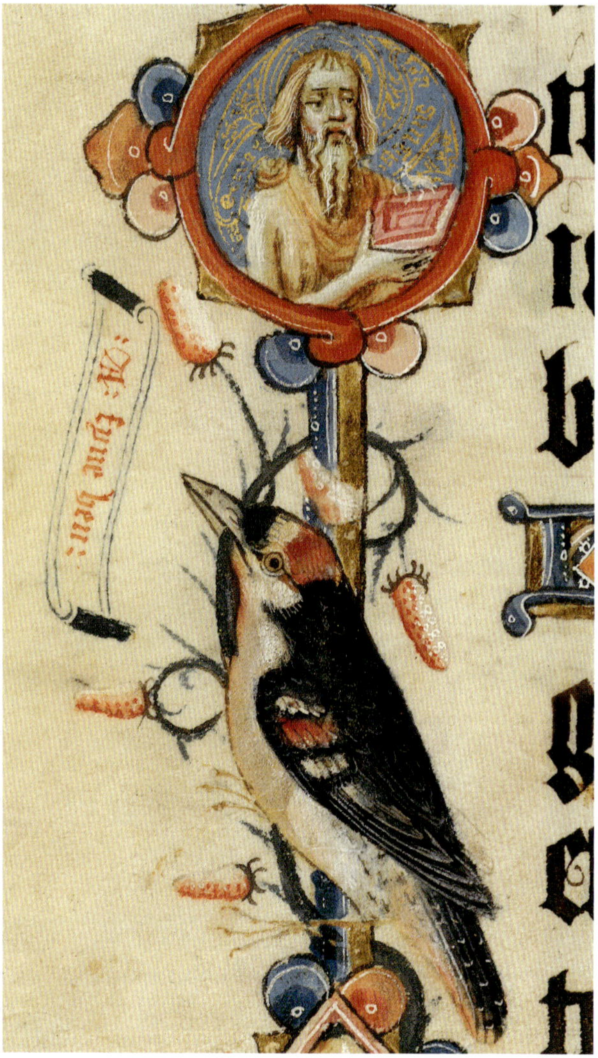

36 *A fyne hen: a bird of uncertain species, possibly derived from a spotted woodpecker and comparable with the subject of picture 16, (p. 384, below).*

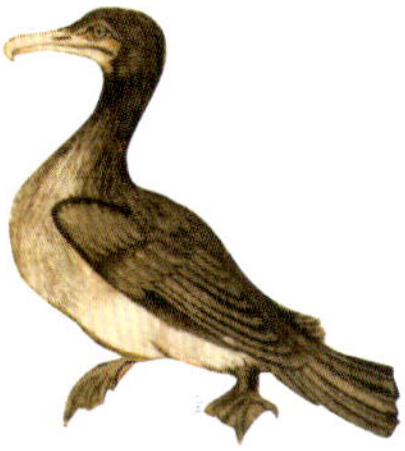

Giovannino de' Grassi sketchbook now in the Biblioteca Civica in Bergamo. Italian inspiration is not unlikely. The content of the Missal betrays the influence of contemporary developments in many parts of Europe, suggesting a wide frame of reference for its principal artist. The rise of naturalism in Italian art during this period has been the subject of numerous studies and links to English art have been explored.

Of the identifiable birds in the series, leaving aside an exotic though well-known species such as the peacock, all are possible in the local context of Dorset though a few, such as the stork (9) and the crane (42), would be passing visitors of great rarity, certainly at the present day. Others, including the shrike (10), the quail (27) and the barnacle goose (44), are very unusual sightings in the area. The models

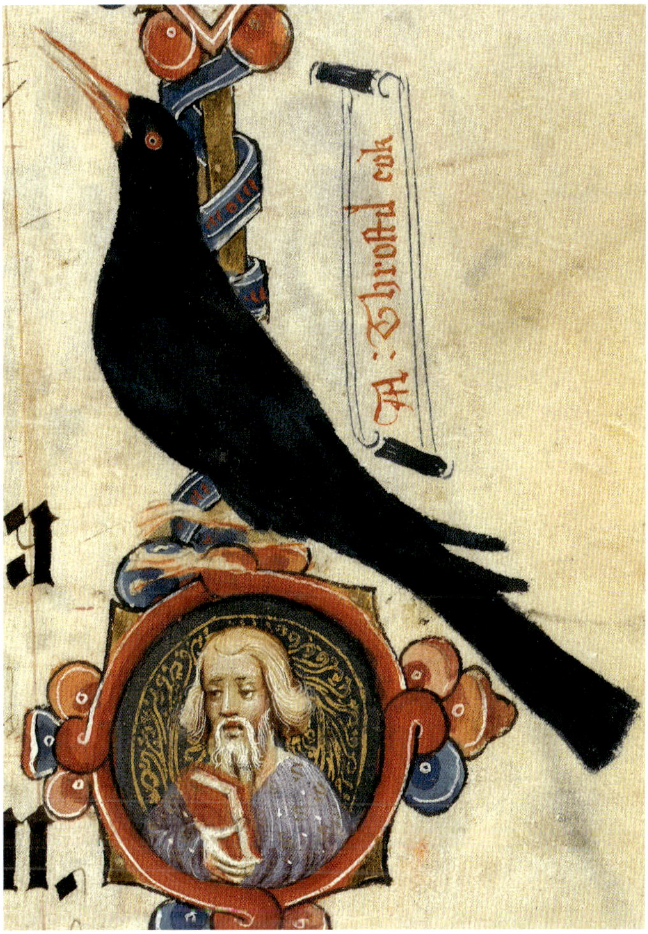


*37 A Throstil cok: the name associated with the thrush is here applied to a blackbird, (p. 385, above).*

used by the artist may, of course, have been observed in some quite other part of the country. Similarly the artist may have played a part in providing the names of the less familiar birds, even if he did not write them out himself.

Professional ornithologists will assess the Sherborne birds in detail for their shapes, attitudes, colours and plumage patterns. Sometimes, inevitably, they will find them wanting. The less experienced will base their reactions upon more general and superficial impressions of colour and shape. Certainly most of them offer plentiful features to allow rapid identification by the interested amateur. Among the most obvious are the robin (32) and, sharing its page, the wren (31), traditionally coupled in folklore as 'God's cock and hen', the one distinguished by its red breast and the other by its unique shape and posture. Colour is also the principal characteristic of the goldfinch (5, 35), the bullfinch (12, 43), the jay (8) and the blackbird (37), though its bill and the rim of its eye are painted red rather than orange. Among the

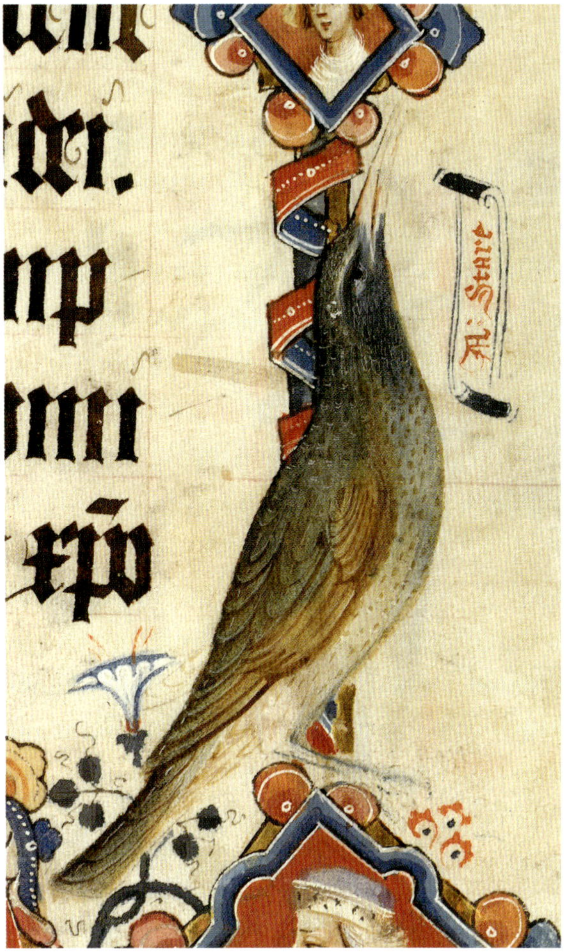


38 *A Stare: a starling, (p. 385, below).*

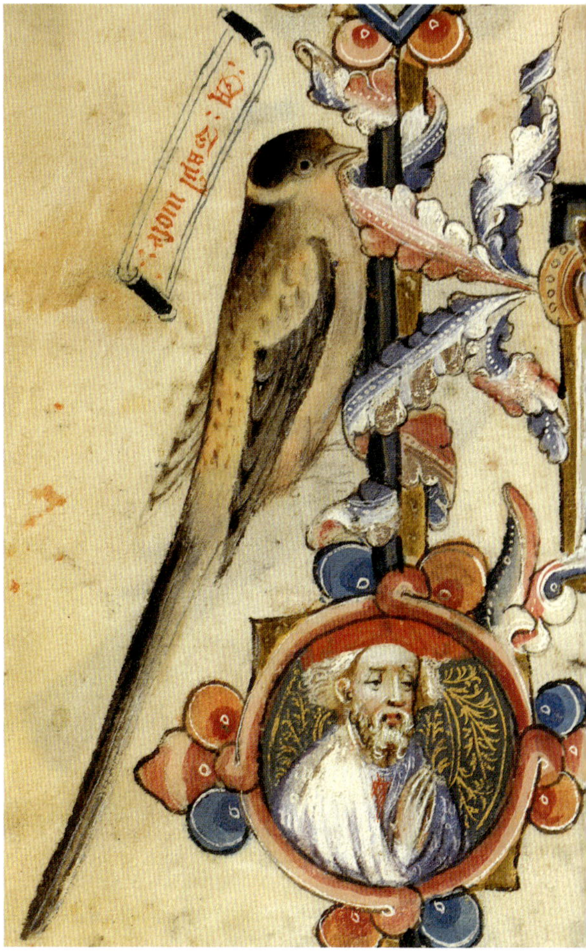

39 *A Tayl mose: a long-tailed tit, (p. 386, above). Enlargement on p. 42.*

less flamboyant species, the hen chaffinch (11) is particularly well rendered, though the cock bird (49) is not quite so successful. The two house sparrows (28, 29), the linnet (45), the fieldfare (47), the skylark (14) with its wispy crest spanning the frame of the page, and the delicately speckled starling (38) are all convincingly suggested, particularly in regard to the colours and patterns of their plumage. Perhaps surprisingly in view of their often striking appearance, the tits are less well portrayed. The first two birds in the series, labelled *mose cok* (2) and *mose hen* (3), are thought to represent the great tit and the bluetit respectively, wrongly regarded as male and female of a single species. However, neither displays the distinctive blue and yellow colouring of these birds, though the general shape of the second is reasonably accurate. The long-tailed tit (39) is more recognisable, if a trifle muted.

However, the coal tit (6), though painted in approximately correct colours, is far too slender for this rather chubby little bird and in fact looks much more like a wagtail (18). All these birds are to be seen in the countryside around the towns and villages of rural England. Today most of them can readily be observed in suburban gardens, where supplementary food and shelter are to be found.

Some of the remaining subjects in the Missal have more specialised natural habitats, but in several cases were obviously observed at first hand by the originator of the studies. A good example is the woodpecker (22). Although at first sight the colouring is perhaps more suggestive of the greater spotted than of the green variety implied by the written name, its shape is extremely well conveyed and it is of the greatest interest to note that the artist has included its extremely long tongue, designed for probing the nests of insects, trailing over the side of its bill and down the adjacent margin. The shrike (10) is similarly well observed, though some of its characteristics, notably the delicate pink colouring of its breast, are more akin to those of the rare lesser grey shrike, native to southern Europe, than to the great grey shrike more usually seen in the British Isles. Among the other land birds, the Sherborne bird painter's particular talent for depicting birds with plumage in varying shades of brown comes into its own in the images of the quail (27) and the hen pheasant (41), both of which are remarkably true to life both in colouring and in form.

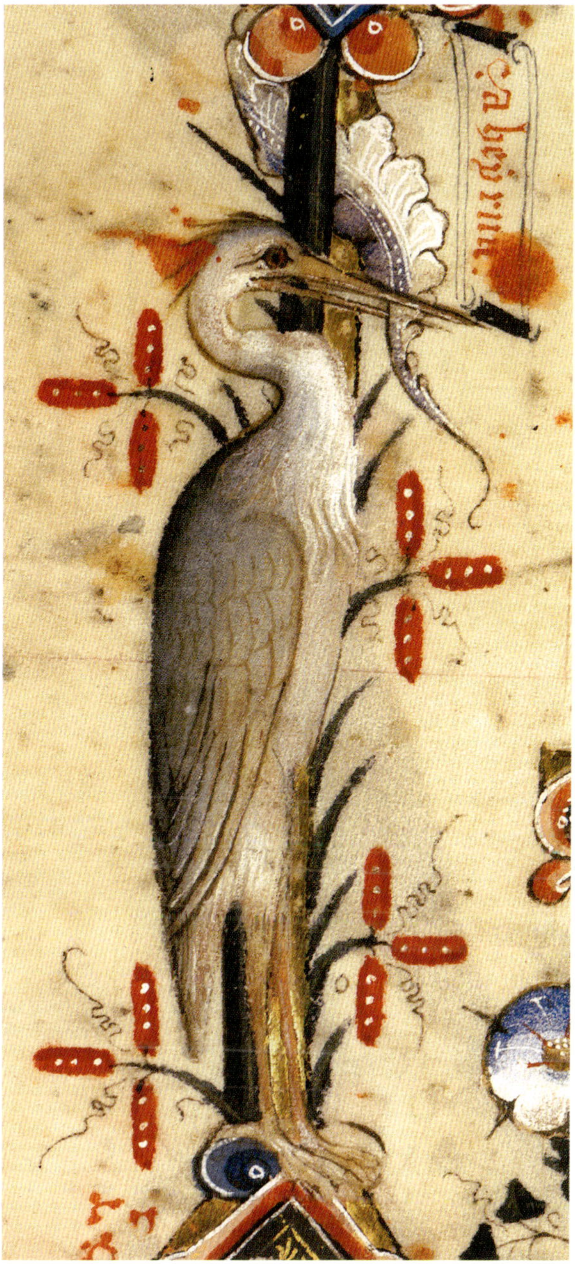

40 *A heyrun: a heron*, (p. 386, *below*).

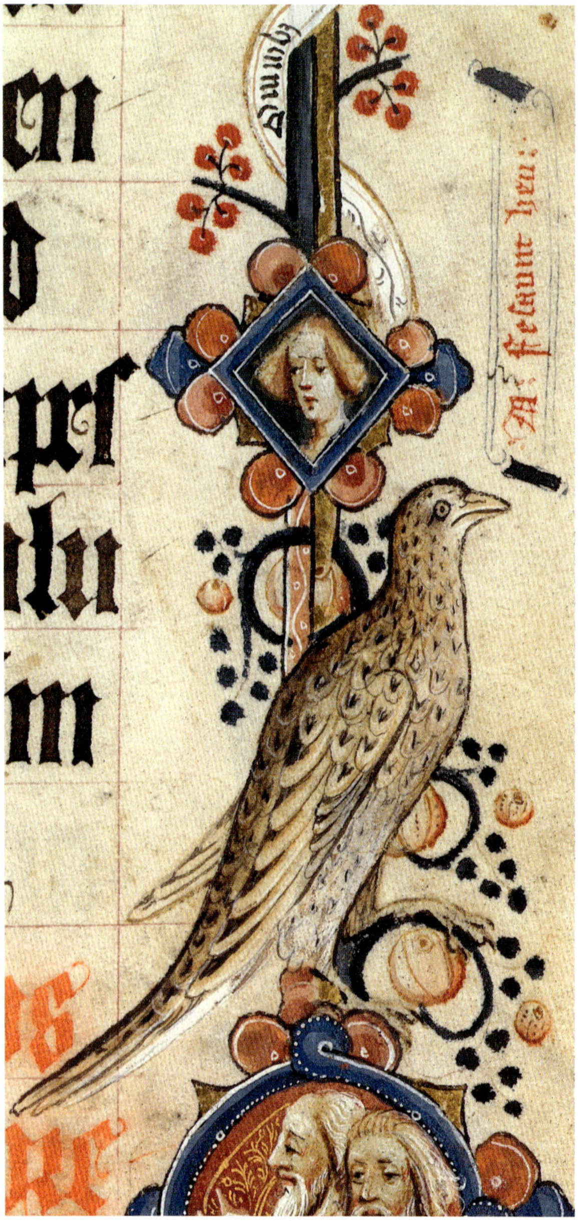


41 *A* Fesaunt hen*: a hen pheasant, (p. 389, above).*

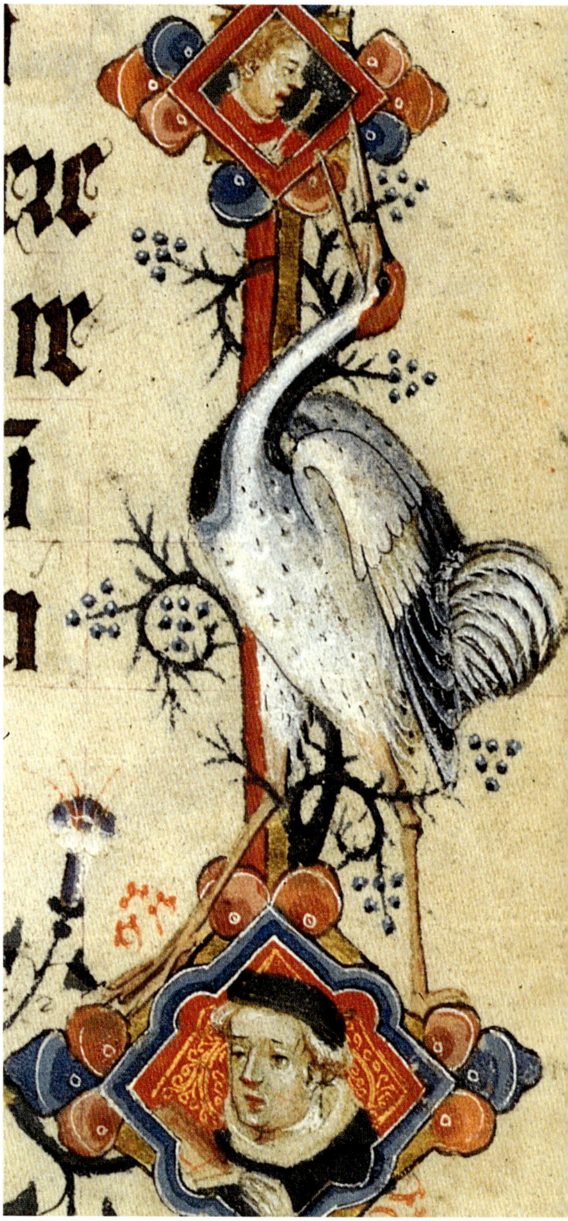

42 Unidentified bird*: a crane, (p. 389, below).*

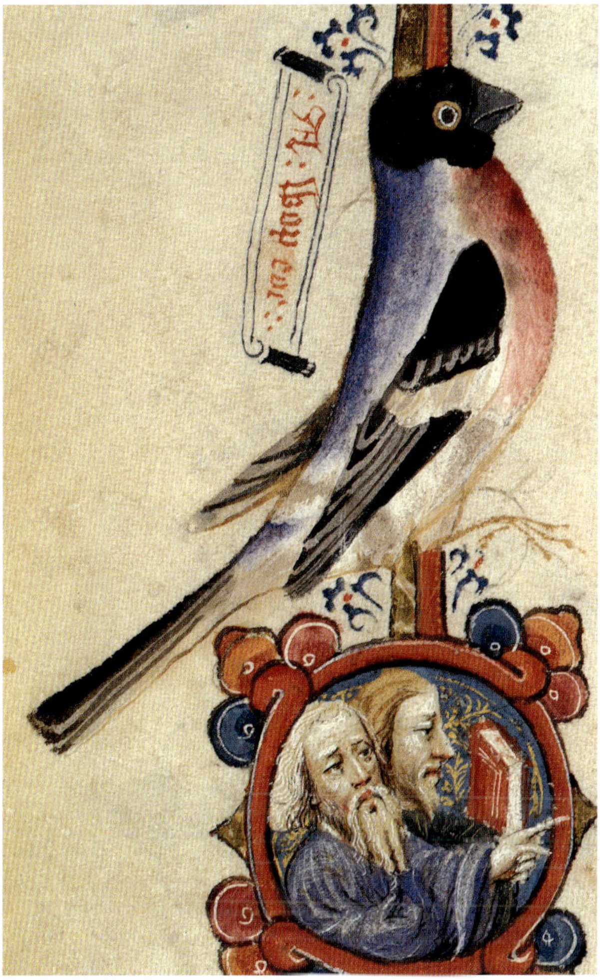


43 *A wop coc: a bullfinch, comparable with picture* 12, (p. 390, *above*).

The remaining birds, comprising more than a quarter of the whole series, are all associated with rivers, wetlands and the sea shore. Among these the kingfisher (33) is noticeably depicted completely out of scale, though once again accurate in form and in distribution of colour, even though its natural brilliancy is much diminished. Two herons appear (40, 50). The first is very well coloured but stands firmly on both feet, grasping a part of the marginal decoration in its beak. The second, though less well defined and unlabelled, is in characteristic one-legged pose and in the course of swallowing an eel. Two totally dissimilar birds are identified as moorhen (7) and moor cock (34). The former name is probably correct, as the bird's most prominent feature is a pair of exceptionally large feet, typical of both moorhen and coot. The characteristic red bill of the bird is lacking and its general colour is brown rather than black, but the shape of

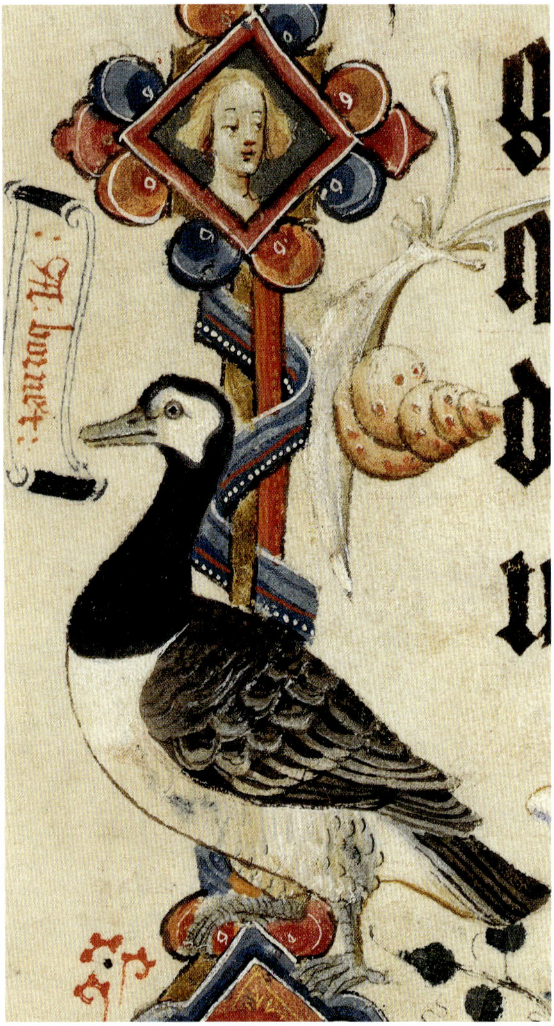


44 *A bornet: a barnacle goose*, (p. 390, below).

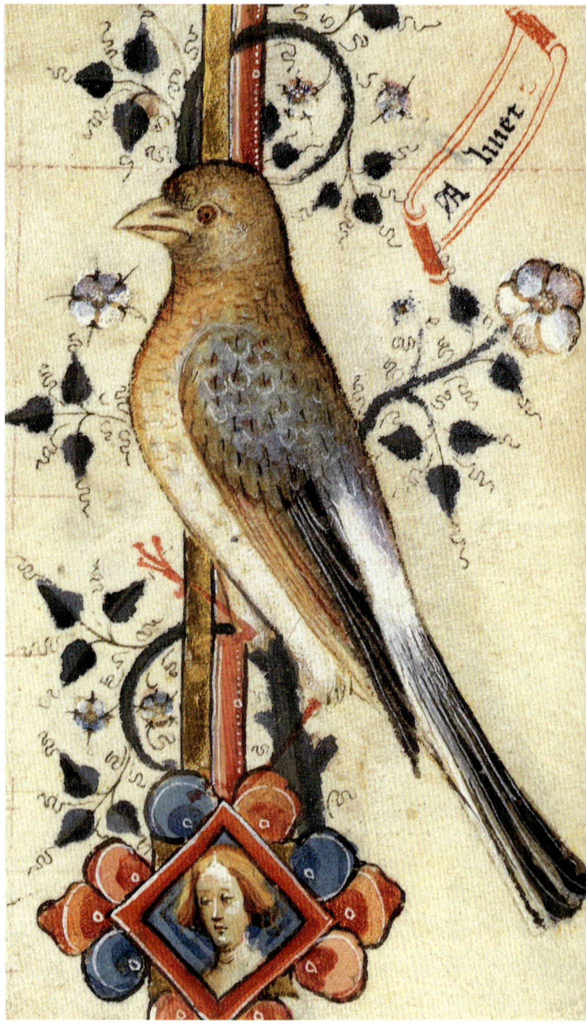


45 *A linet: a linnet*, (p. 391, above).

the head, the white edging of the wing and the white patch beneath the tail are all present. Maybe the model was an immature bird. The latter is of a different type altogether and its shape suggests a wader. The long, straight bill and the distinctive feather patterns are more or less consistent with those of the godwit, different varieties of which would almost certainly not have been distinguished in the early 15th century. Two further waders, the snipe (23) and the woodcock (25), are also included, the latter unnamed but unmistakable.

Three ducks and two geese appear. The first is a shelduck (17), followed by a pair of teal (19, 21). The colourful and sharply defined markings of the

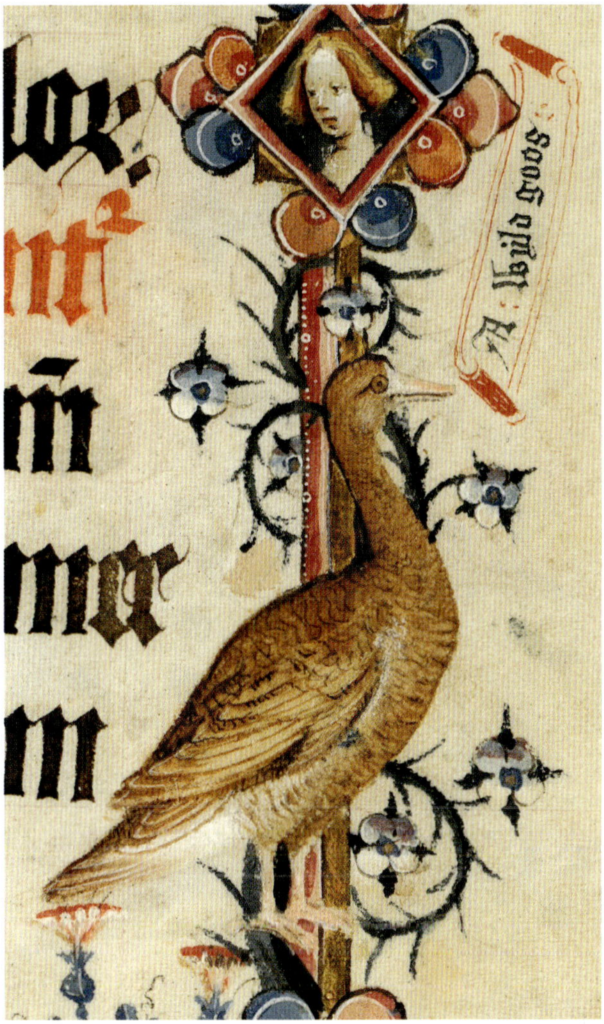


46 *A wyld goos: possibly a greylag,* (p. 391, *below*).

shelduck are not well rendered unless here too the model was a juvenile. The teal drake is better marked but the hen could equally well be a hen mallard. The first of the geese (44) is labelled as a *bornet*, the name suggesting that the subject might a brent goose. This is, however, an extremely well observed barnacle goose, again reflecting contemporary inability to distinguish between apparently similar species. The second goose is simply designated *wyld* (46). Its warm brown colouring is not immediately characteristic of any species, though the artist is most likely to have had the fairly widespread greylag in mind.

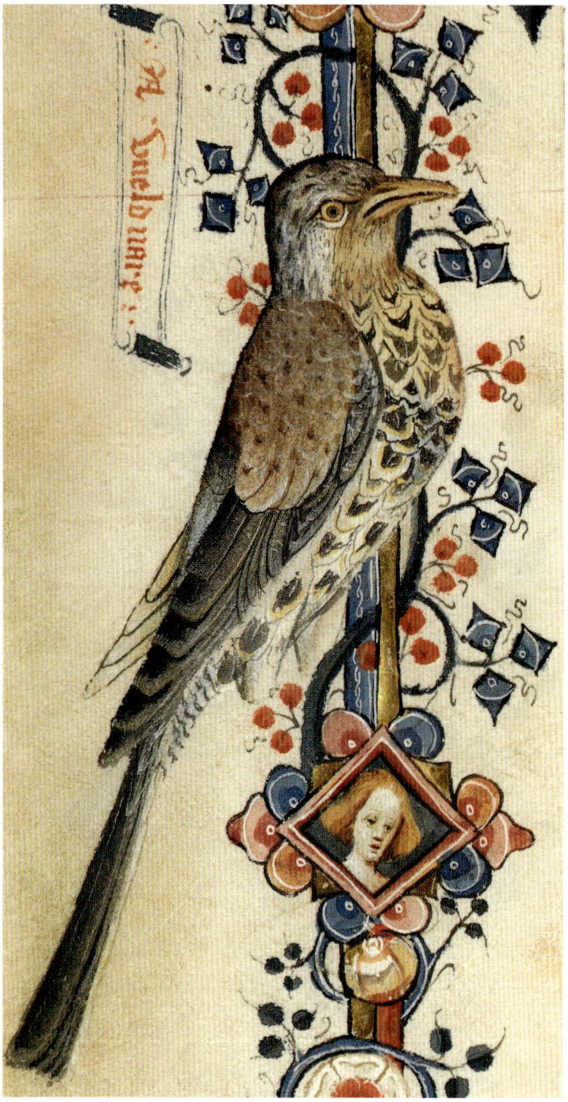

*47 A vuelduare: a fieldfare, (p. 392, above). Enlargement on p. 56.*

Finally there are three seabirds, a cormorant (13), a gannet (15) and a gull (48). Today the first of these is a familiar visitor to inland waters and may also be sighted around the whole of the English coastline. The artist has rightly stressed its large feet, heavy hooked bill and dark colouring, though again the colour could indicate an immature bird. His gannet is correctly shaped, but in place of the dazzling white plumage of the adult bird, contrasting dramatically with its black wing tips and ochre-coloured head, he has given it the much duller speckled brown of a juvenile bird. Nowadays the gannet's major breeding sites are concentrated in the north of the British Isles. However, it would seem that during

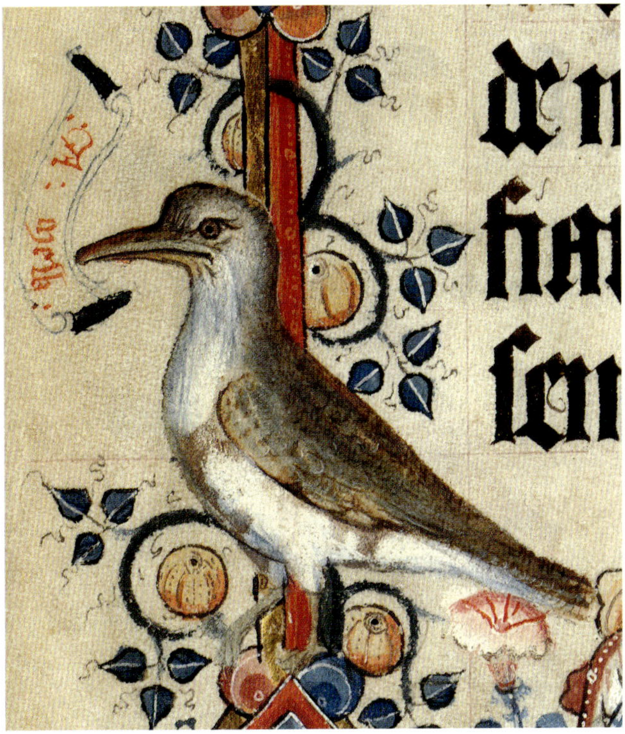

48 *A mew: a seagull,* (p. 392, *below*).

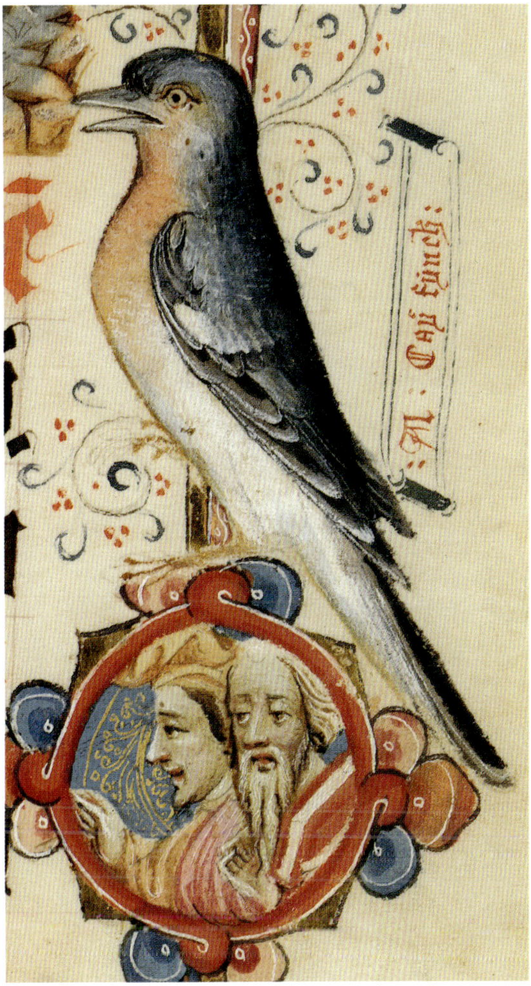


49 *A Cay fynch: a chaffinch, probably intended as the male of the species seen in picture* 11 (p. 393, *above*).

the Middle Ages the bird was a noted resident of Lundy Island in the Bristol Channel, less than a hundred miles from Sherborne, so the model for this image could have been found fairly locally. The gull seems also to be a juvenile, perhaps of the herring or the black-backed gull.

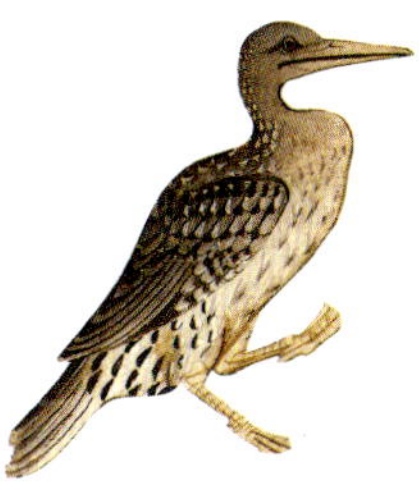

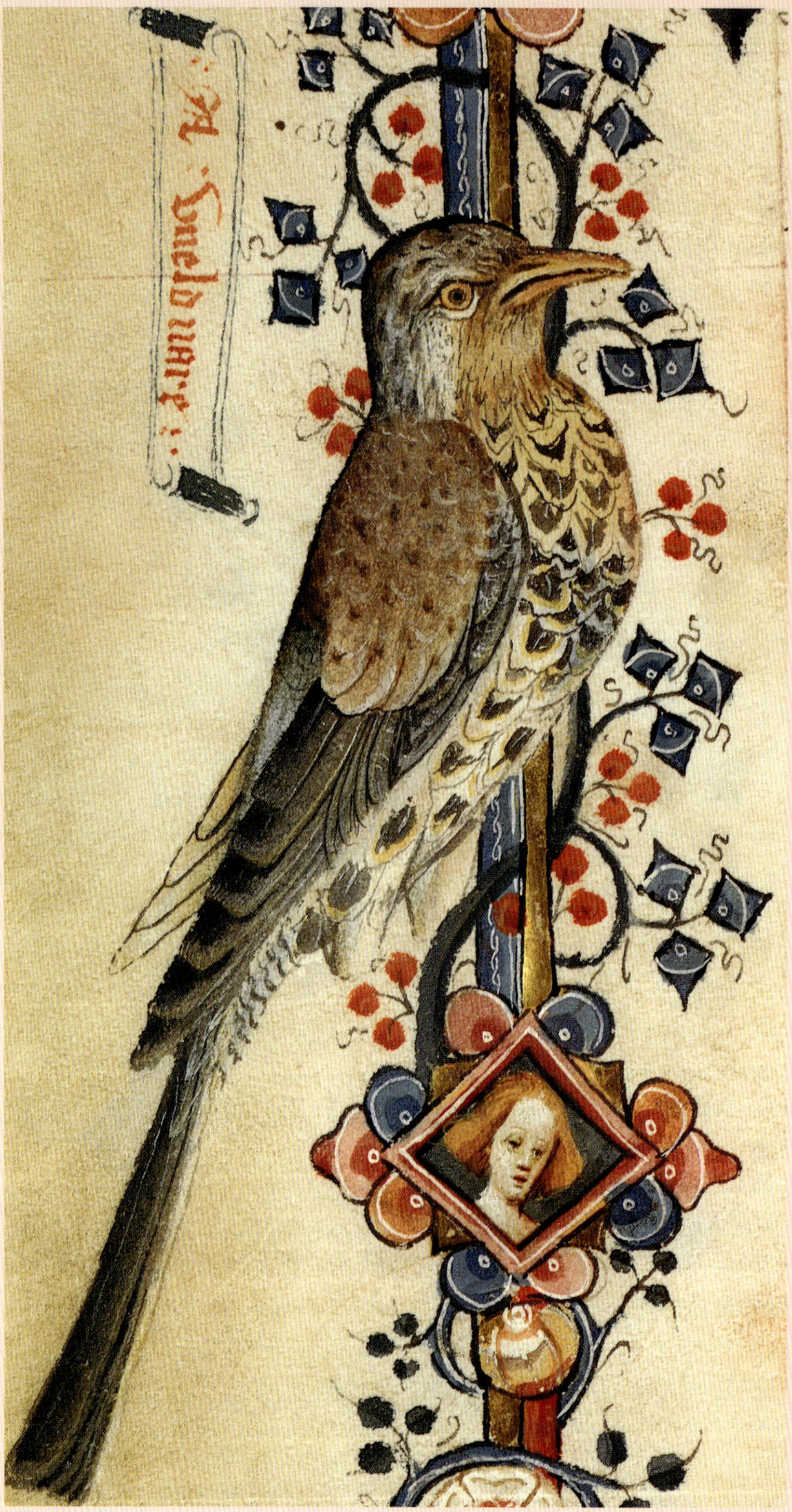

# THE STUDY OF THE BIRDS

This is the first time that the birds of the Sherborne Missal have been reproduced as a complete series in colour and in readily accessible form. The manuscript, presumably until then kept at Sherborne, disappeared from sight in the 16th century, at the time of the Reformation, and later was for many years the property of a succession of private collectors in France. It was brought back to England at the end of the 18th century and in 1800 was purchased for the library of the Dukes of Northumberland. Thereafter its existence was known only to a privileged few before it was lent for exhibition in London, at the Society of Antiquaries, in 1896 by the 6th Duke. His successor, the 8th Duke, commissioned J.A. Herbert of the British Museum to make a study of it and this was published in 1920. A selection of birds, together with a transcript of the names and some modern parallels, was included, though Herbert endearingly confessed: 'The present writer's equipment as a naturalist is too meagre to warrant him in attempting to identify the remainder. He has little doubt, however, that this could be done, and would be worth doing.' Although since then the manuscript has featured in every major discussion of English medieval painting, taking its proper place as one of the supreme examples of the illuminator's art, specialised interest in the birds was not seriously re-awakened until about 1980.

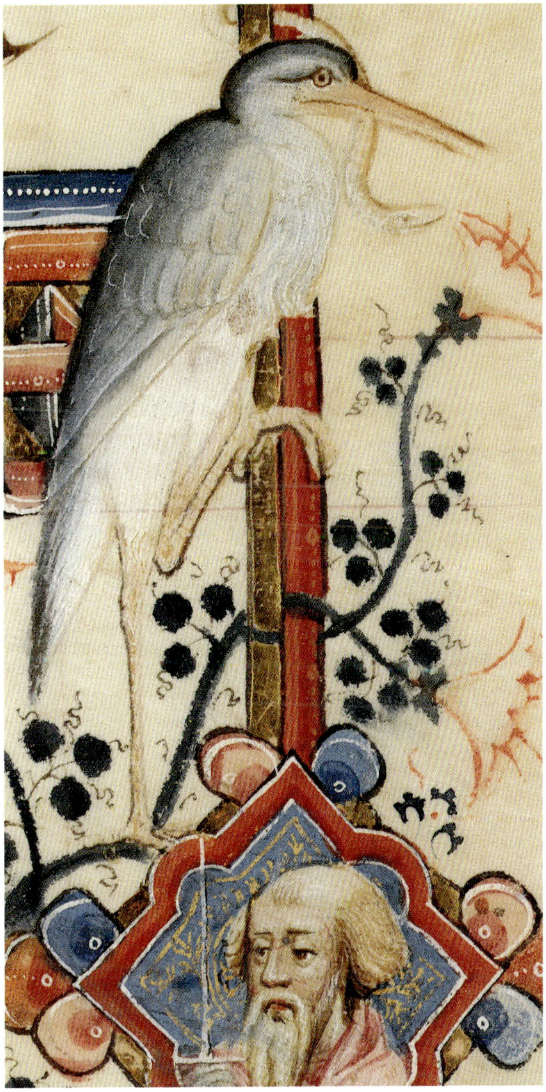

*50 Unidentified bird: a heron, to be compared with the image on picture 40, (p. 393, below).*

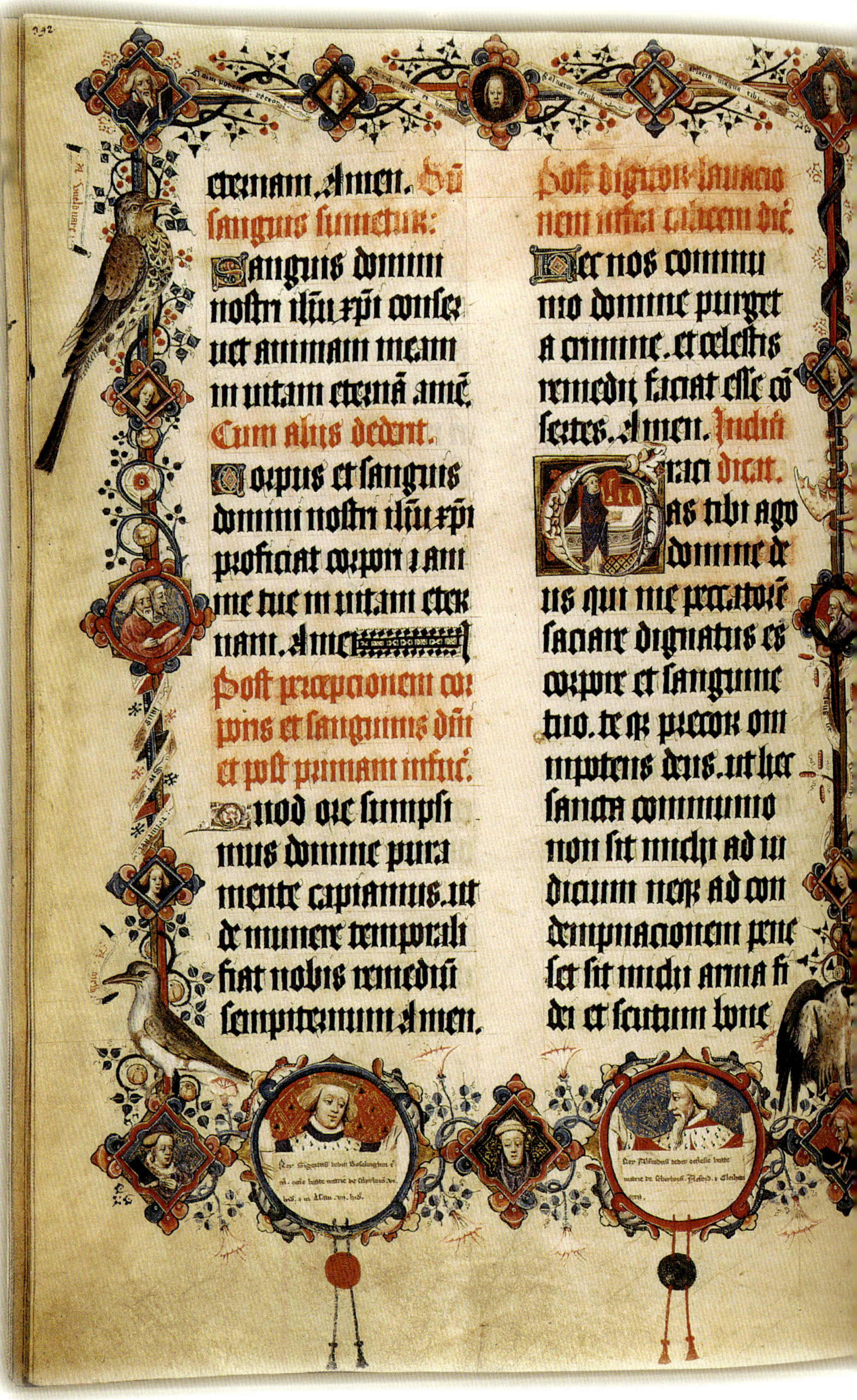
242

eternam. Amen. Dum sanguis sumetur:
Sanguis domini nostri ihesu christi conservet animam meam in vitam eternam amen.
Cum aliis dederit.
Corpus et sanguis domini nostri ihesu christi proficiat corpori et anime tue in vitam eternam. Amen.
Post percepcionem corporis et sanguinis domini et post primam infusionem.
Quod ore sumpsimus domine pura mente capiamus. ut de munere temporali fiat nobis remedium sempiternum. Amen.

Post digitorum lavacionem infusi calicem dicat.
Hec nos communio domine purget a crimine. et celestis remedii faciat esse consortes. Amen. Inclinatus dicat.
Gracias tibi ago domine deus qui me peccatorem saciare dignatus es corpore et sanguine tuo. te ergo precor omnipotens deus. ut hec sancta communio non sit michi ad iudicium neque ad condempnacionem pro scelere sit michi arma fidei et scutum bone

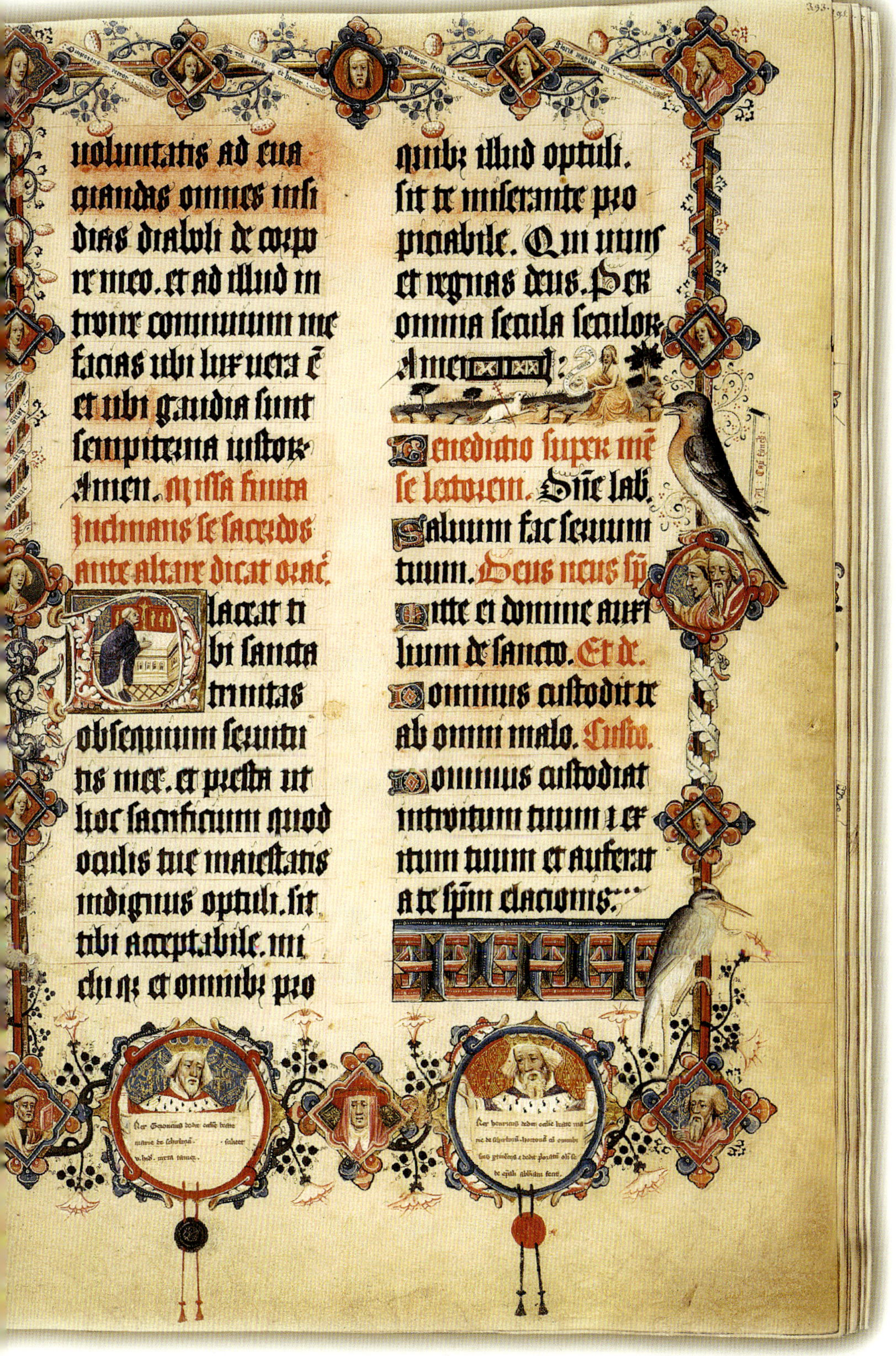

51 *An opening from the manuscript, with decoration showing various royal benefactors. The marginal birds are the fieldfare, the seagull, the chaffinch and the heron, with an additional crane included for purely ornamental reasons at the foot of the left-hand page (pp. 392–3).*

Scholarly requests for access to the manuscript, then kept at Alnwick Castle, in order to study them were among the reasons which inspired the 10th Duke to deposit the Missal on indefinite loan in the British Library, where it could be professionally supervised and cared for, in 1983. On the death of the 11th Duke, its sale to the nation was negotiated.

A survey of existing literature suggests that about a quarter of the birds have never before been reproduced. Others have been published in black and white rather than in colour. Available reproductions have to be sought in a number of different places, including Herbert's book, which is a rarity in its own right. Access to the original manuscript is limited by its great value and vulnerability to excessive handling. Although it is consistently on exhibition in the British Library's galleries, only two pages can be visible at any one time and these are only occasionally chosen to feature the birds, such is the richness of the Missal's contents.

Although this writer cannot claim to be a specialist in the study of Middle English and echoes Herbert's meagre equipment as a naturalist, she has enjoyed the benefits of the many advances in the understanding of the manuscript which have resulted from recent work by linguists and ornithologists. The publication of these images as a coherent entity will help to clarify their place in the scheme of the Sherborne Missal and in the philosophy that produced it.

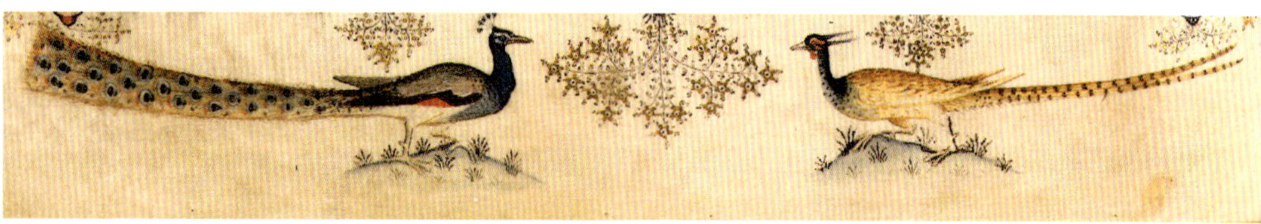

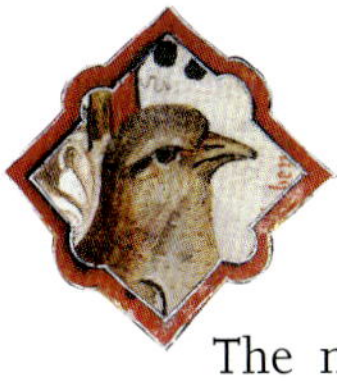

# SUGGESTIONS FOR FURTHER READING

The manuscript as a whole is described and illustrated in detail in Janet Backhouse, *The Sherborne Missal*, The British Library, London, 1999.

A preliminary survey of the birds is given in W.B. Yapp, 'The Birds of the Sherborne Missal', *Proceedings of the Dorset Natural History and Archaeological Society*, 104 (1982), pp. 5-15. The same issue contains E.D.V. Prendergast, 'Dorset Names for Birds', pp. 33-7.

Vernacular bird names have attracted extensive study. A useful source, with bibliography, is W.B. Lockwood, *The Oxford Book of British Bird Names*, Oxford University Press, 1984. A second edition of this book, re-titled *The Oxford Dictionary of British Bird Names*, 1993, incorporates material from the Sherborne Missal.

A general introduction to birds in manuscripts is provided by Brunsdon Yapp, *Birds in Medieval Manuscripts*, The British Library, London, 1981. For bestiary illustrations see the relevant sections in Ann Payne, *Medieval Beasts*, The British Library, London, 1990. The birds in the Pepysian Sketchbook are all reproduced in M.R. James, 'An English Medieval Sketchbook, No. 1916 in the Pepysian Library, Magdalene College, Cambridge', *The Walpole Society*, xiii (1921-5), pp. 1-77 and pls. x-xiii. This manuscript and the Italian material are all included in R.W. Scheller, *A Survey of Medieval Model Books*, Haarlem, 1963.

More generally see Francis Klingender, *Animals in art and thought to the end of the Middle Ages*, Routledge and Kegan Paul, London, 1971

Books on British birds are plentiful and readers are likely to have their own favourite sources. For the area which produced the Sherborne Missal, reference should be made to E.D.V. Prendergast and I.V. Boys, *The Birds of Dorest*, David and Charles, Newton Abbot, 1983. More generally see Francis Klingender, *Animals in art and thought to the end of the Middle Ages*, Routledge and Kegan Paul, London, 1971.

A very enjoyable survey of historical attitudes to birds is provided by Francesca Greenoak, *British Birds: their Folklore, Names and Literature*, Christopher Helm/ A & C Black, London, 1997.

# INDEX OF BIRD NAMES

*Numbers in italics refer to illustration numbers*

## INDEX OF BIRD NAMES



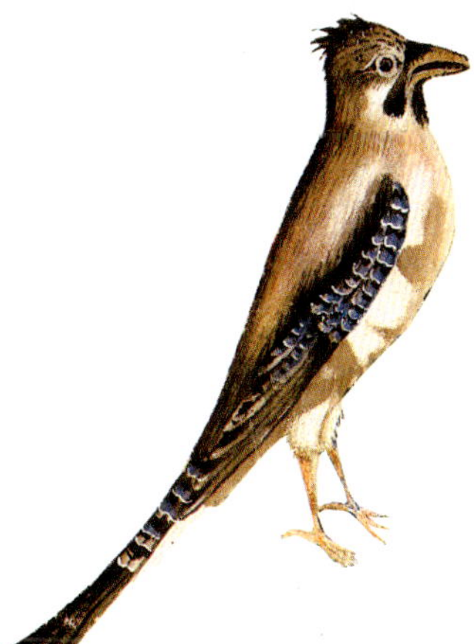

## THE AUTHOR

Janet Backhouse is an internationally respected manuscript expert and former Curator of Illuminated Manuscripts at The British Library. She is the author of many books on the subject, including: *Medieval Rural Life in the Luttrell Psalter* (2000), *The Illuminated Page: Ten Centuries of Manuscript Painting* (1997), *The Hastings Hours* (1996), *The Lindisfarne Gospels: A Masterpiece of Book Painting* (1995), *The Isabella Breviary* (1993), *The Bedford Hours* (1990), *The Luttrell Psalter* (1989), *The Becket Leaves* (co-author, 1988), *Books of Hours* (1985), *The Lindisfarne Gospels* (1981), and *The Illuminated Manuscript* (1979). She has also collaborated on a number of exhibition catalogues, including *The Making of England* (1991), *The Golden Age of Anglo-Saxon Art* (1984), and *Renaissance Painting in Manuscripts* (1984).

| | |
|---|---|
| *Front Cover Illustration:* | *A Cayfynch hen: a hen chaffinch (p. 367, below).* |
| *Half-title Page:* | *The swan used as a livery badge (p. 365, detail).* |
| *Frontispiece:* | *Easter Sunday: the Resurrection (p. 216).* |
| *Title Page:* | *Image of the artist, John Siferwas, beside the arms and badge of Henry V as Prince of Wales (p. 81, detail).* |
| *Back Cover:* | *A Wrenne: a wren (p.382, above).* |

First published 2001 by
The British Library
96 Euston Road
London NW1 2DB



British Library Cataloguing in Publication Data
A catalogue record for this book is available from The British Library

ISBN 0 7123 4705 4
Designed and typeset by Crayon Design, Stoke Row, Henley-on-Thames
Colour origination by Crayon Design and South Sea International Press
Printed in Hong Kong by South Sea International Press